The Most Horrible Mayhem

by John S. Gruse

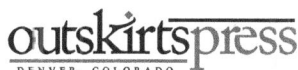

DENVER, COLORADO

The Most Horrible Mayhem
All Rights Reserved.
Copyright © 2014 John S. Gruse
v2.0

Front cover: "Memory" by John S. Gruse
Back cover: "Fleur Du Mal" by John S. Gruse

Outskirts Press, Inc.
http://www.outskirtspress.com

ISBN: 978-1-4787-0878-0

Outskirts Press and the "OP" logo are trademarks belonging to Outskirts Press, Inc.

PRINTED IN THE UNITED STATES OF AMERICA

VISITATION

She leaned forward with gentle heat
And eyes hidden in her hair.
Monochrome words cannot describe
The delerium of her total presence.

In the dazzling light of a first love
Her humid kisses, breathing with musk,
Filled me with gold,
But stole from me my strength.

Suddenly, with a lacerating tongue,
She cut the bond between us,
And soft talons
Laid open my heart.

Rising, she straightened herself
And floated away,
Leaving behind the luminous haze
Of her lethal perfume.

I shoulder the burden she left,
A dogged widower
To an uncaring phantom
Whose memory still runs in my veins.

Lilith, I believe, I have known. I've written her name on everything.

This book is a catalog of some of her many monstrous children, as I perceive them. My dreams were long ago infected by these horrors, bequeathed to me by their faithless mother, and I believe I've been most kind in my interpretation of their forms.

This book is about the decay of the perfect illusion, when planted in a bed of fetid memories.

This is an imagined retelling of the legend of Lilith With The Long Hair, a character found primarily in Jewish biblical lore. Any resemblences to persons living or dead are purely coincidental.

To La Belle Dame Sans Merci

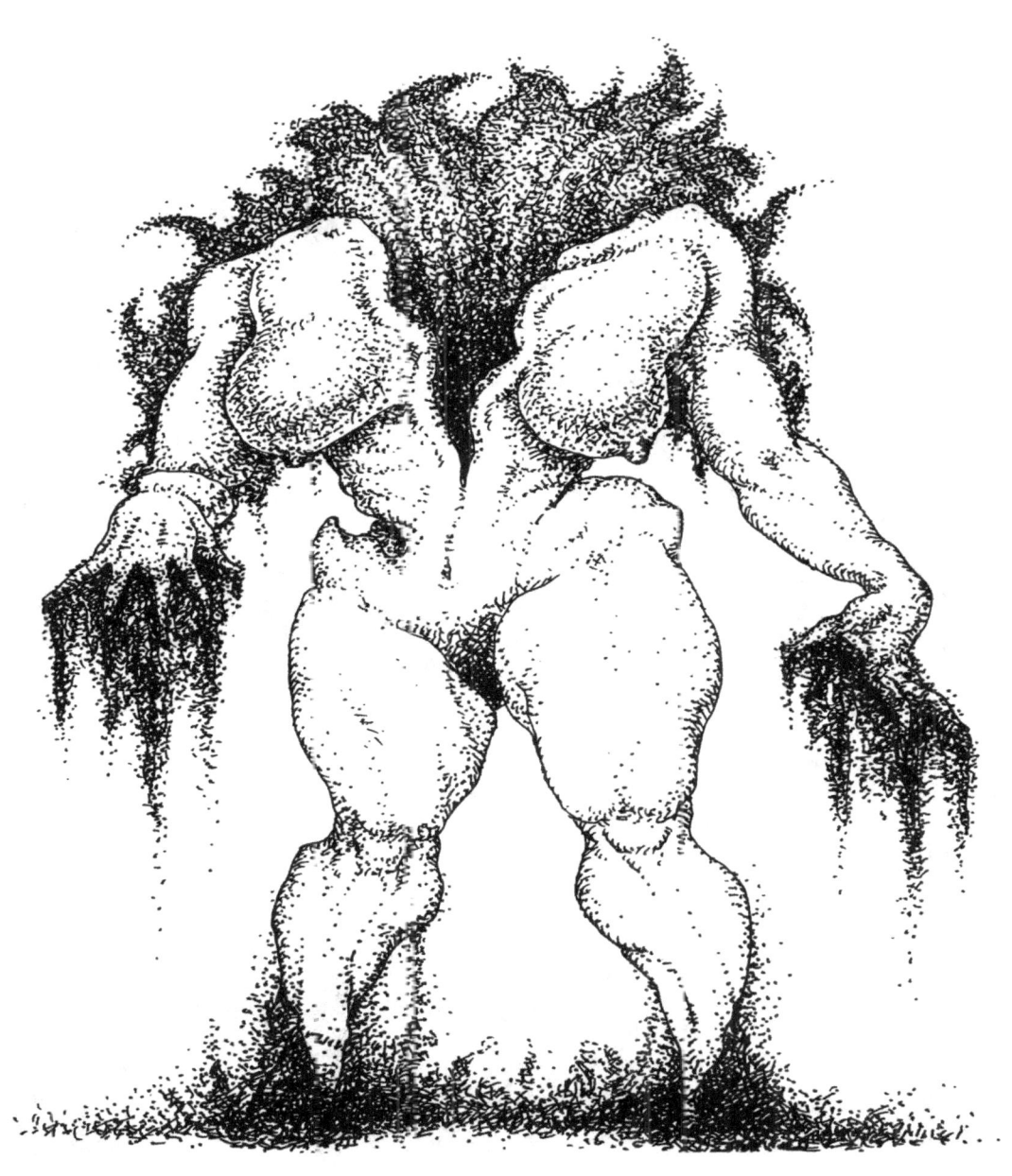

Swaying in my vision,

Her body throws out horror.

"Oh, it's not that bad", she says,

Unblushing.

The most horrible mayhem

Merely keeps her at bay.

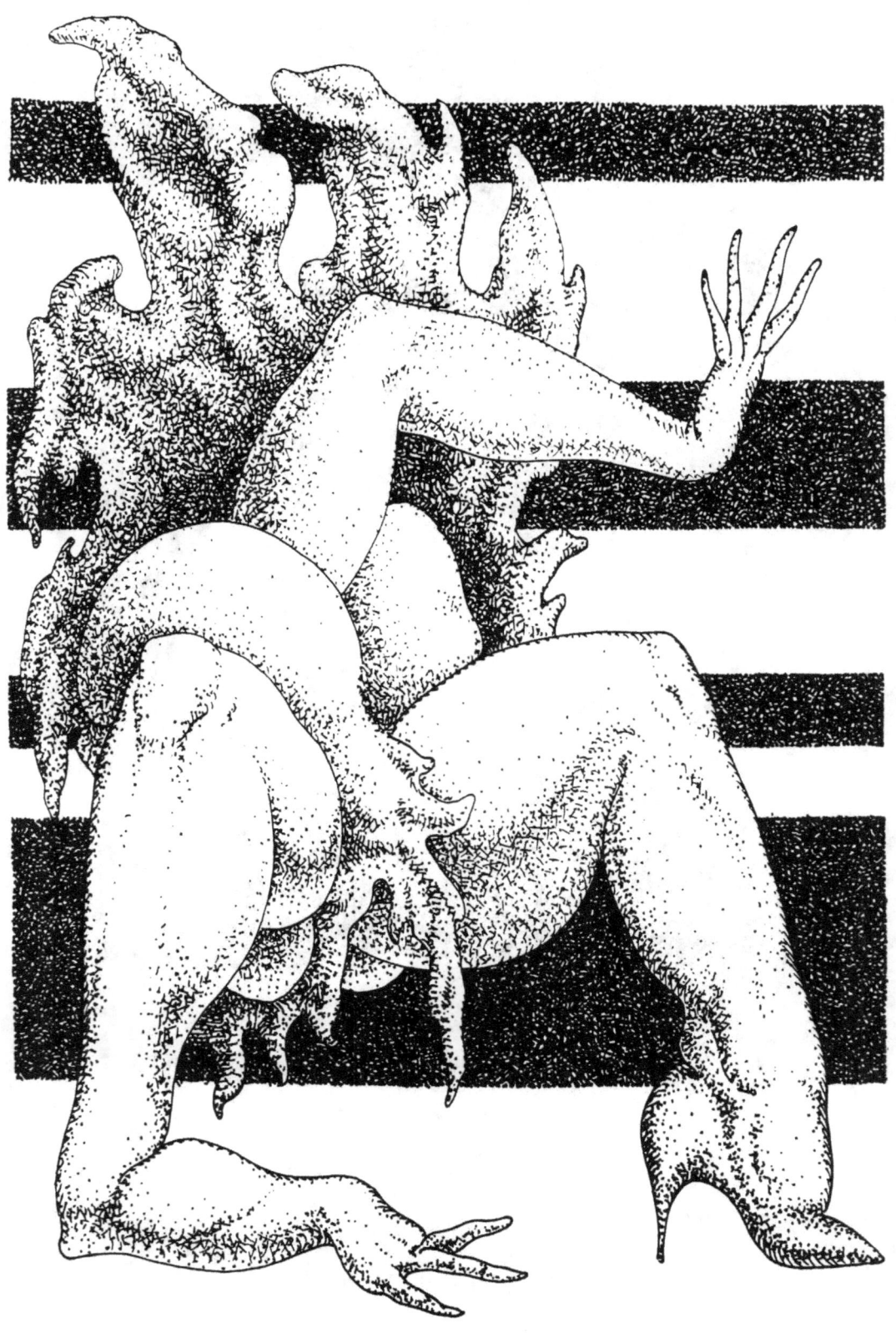

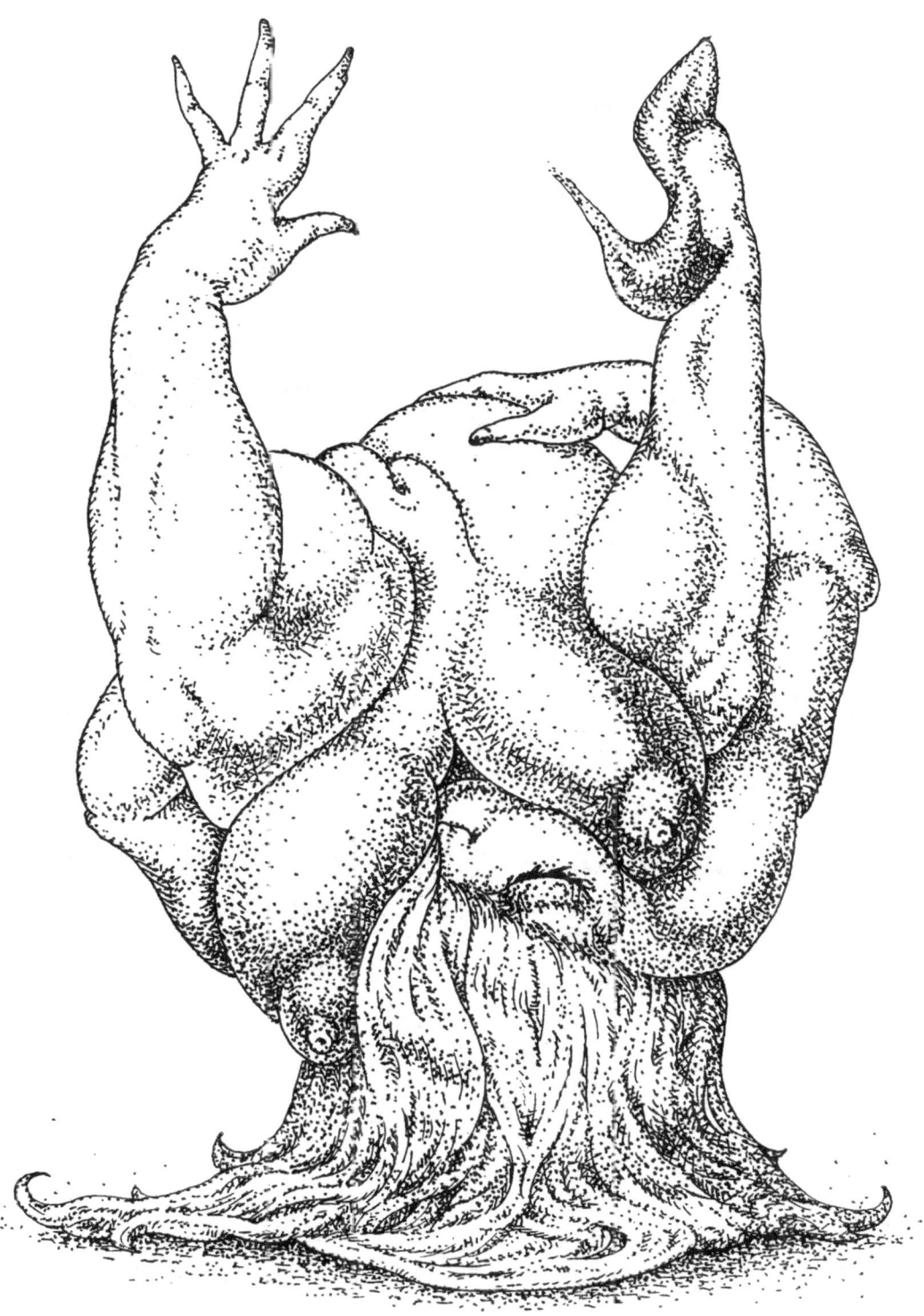

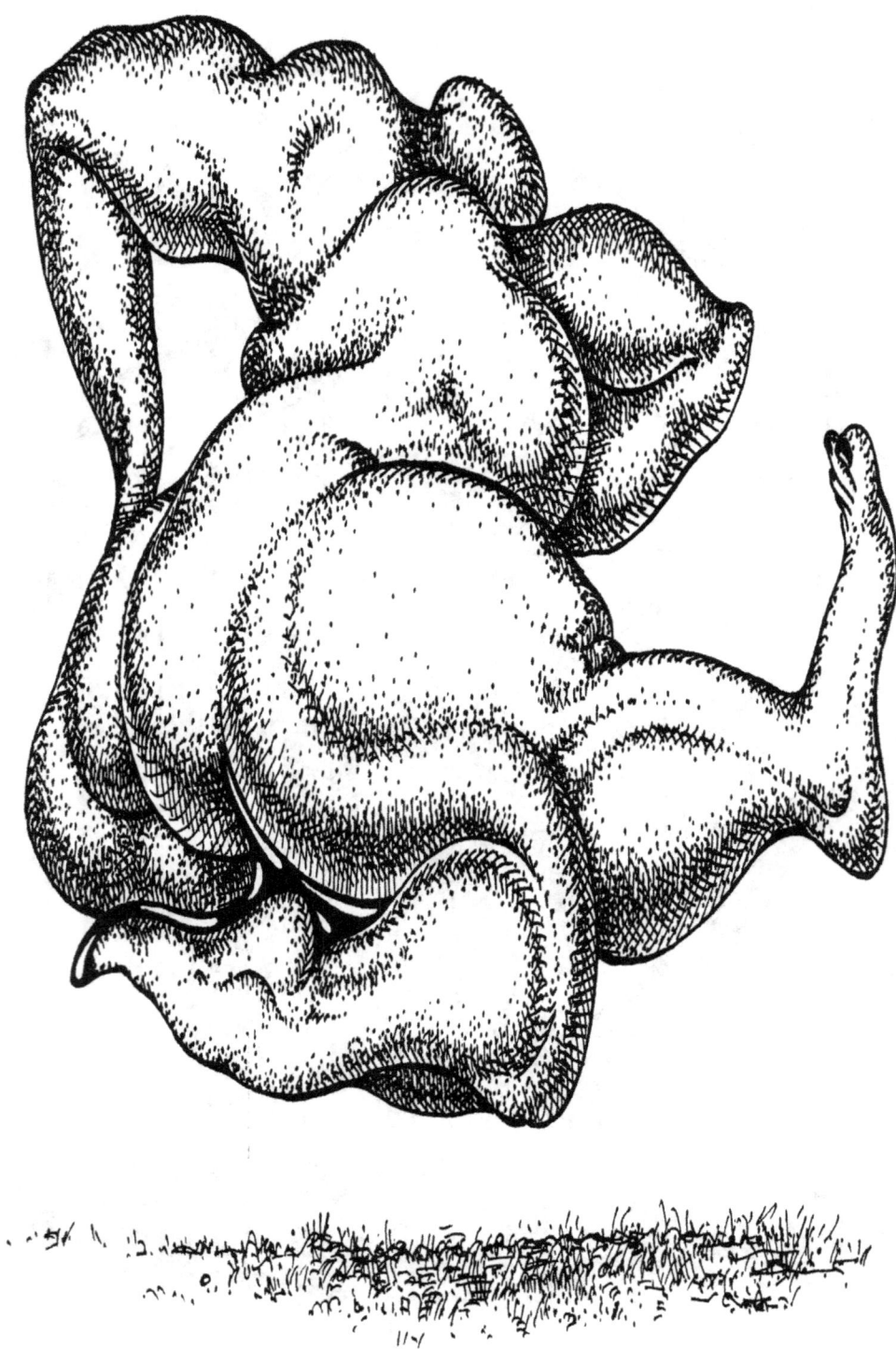

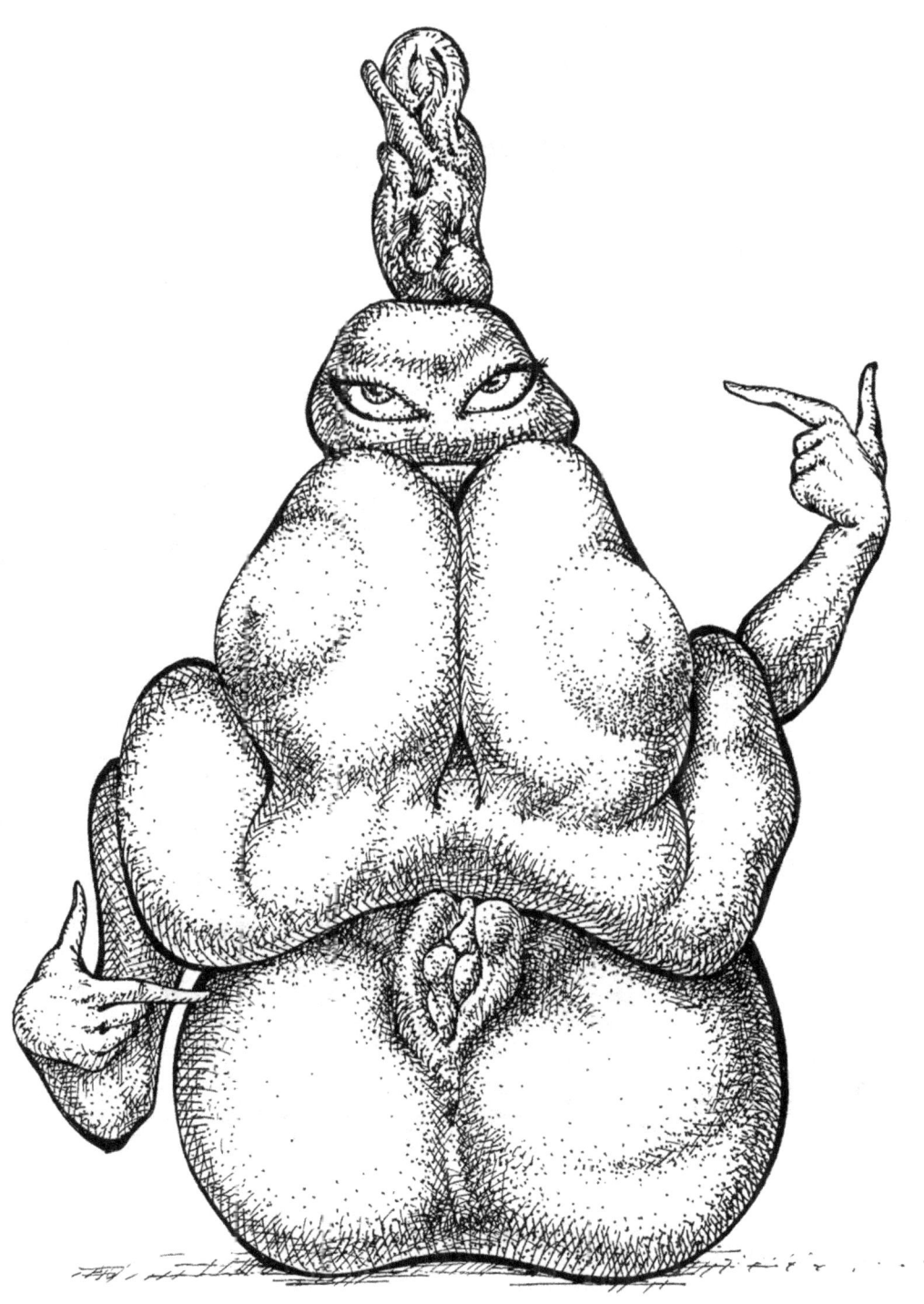

5

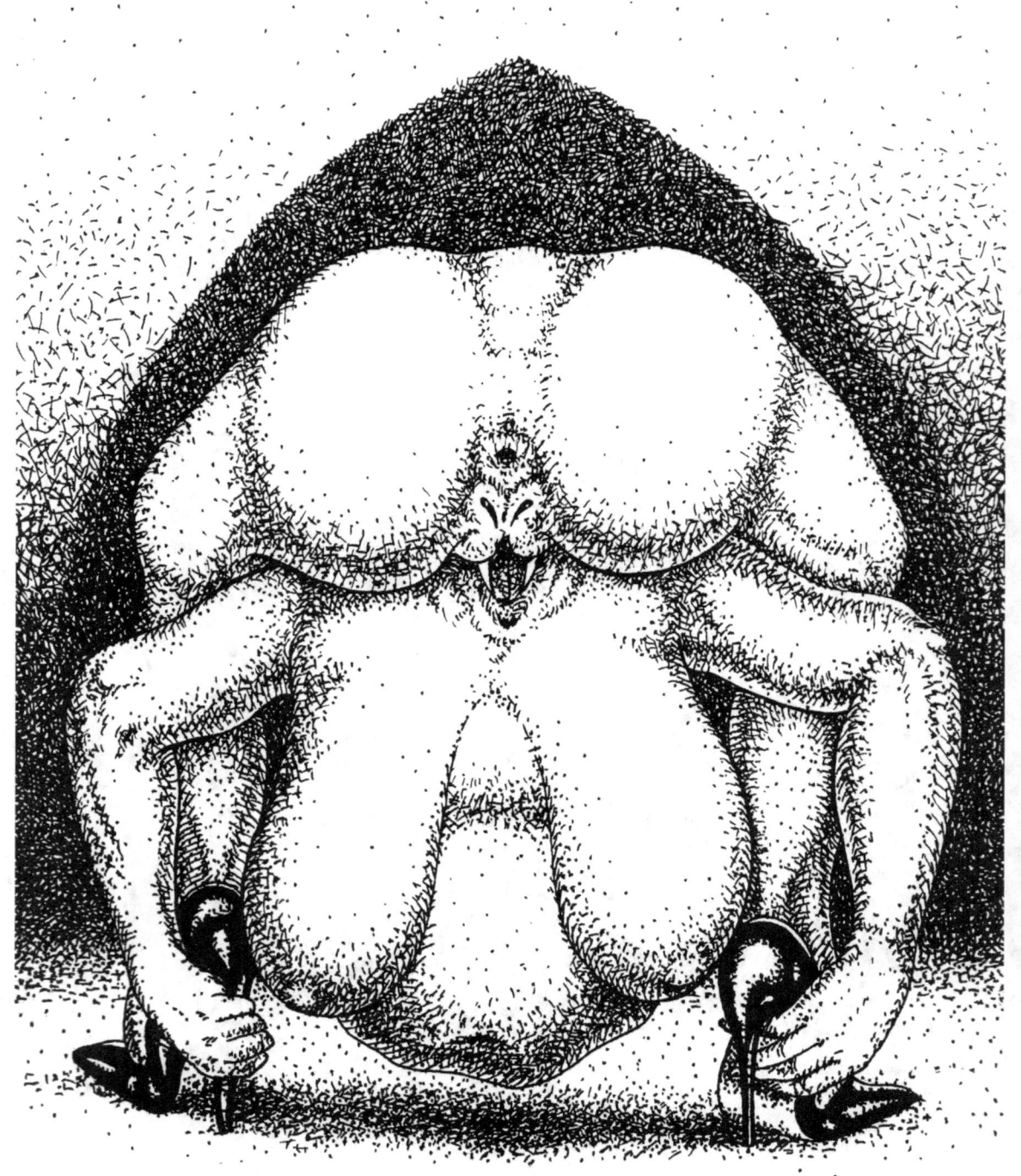

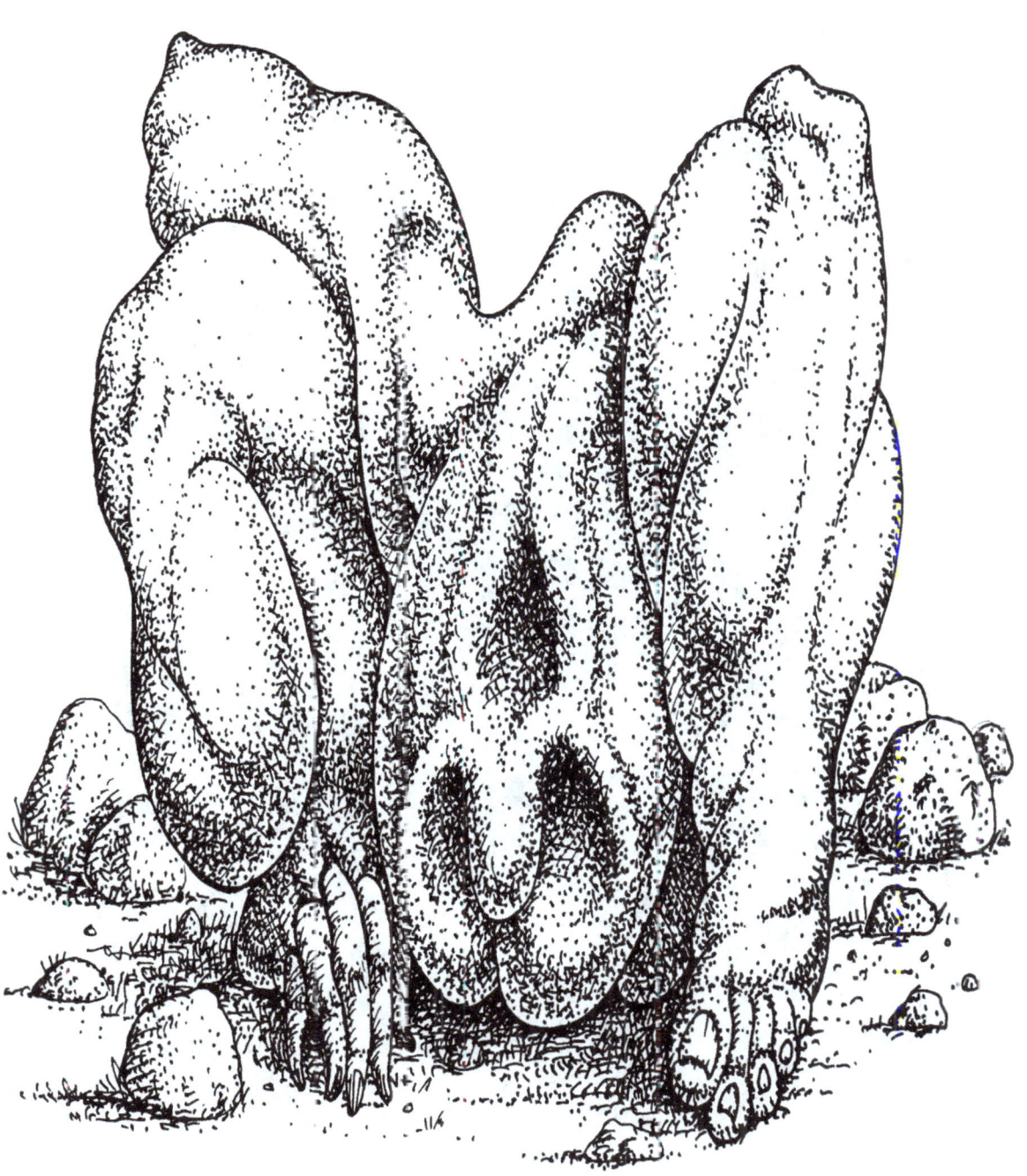

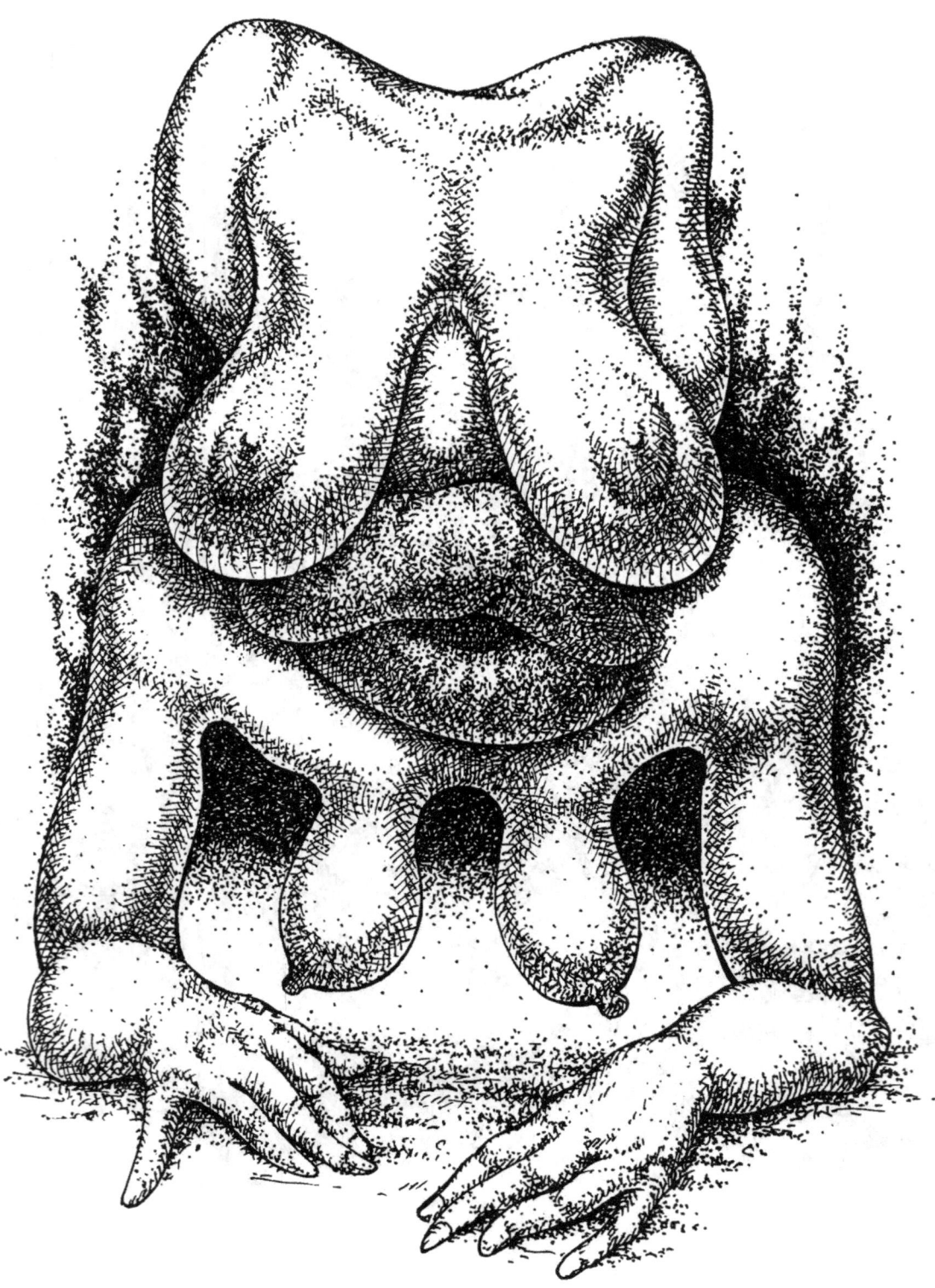

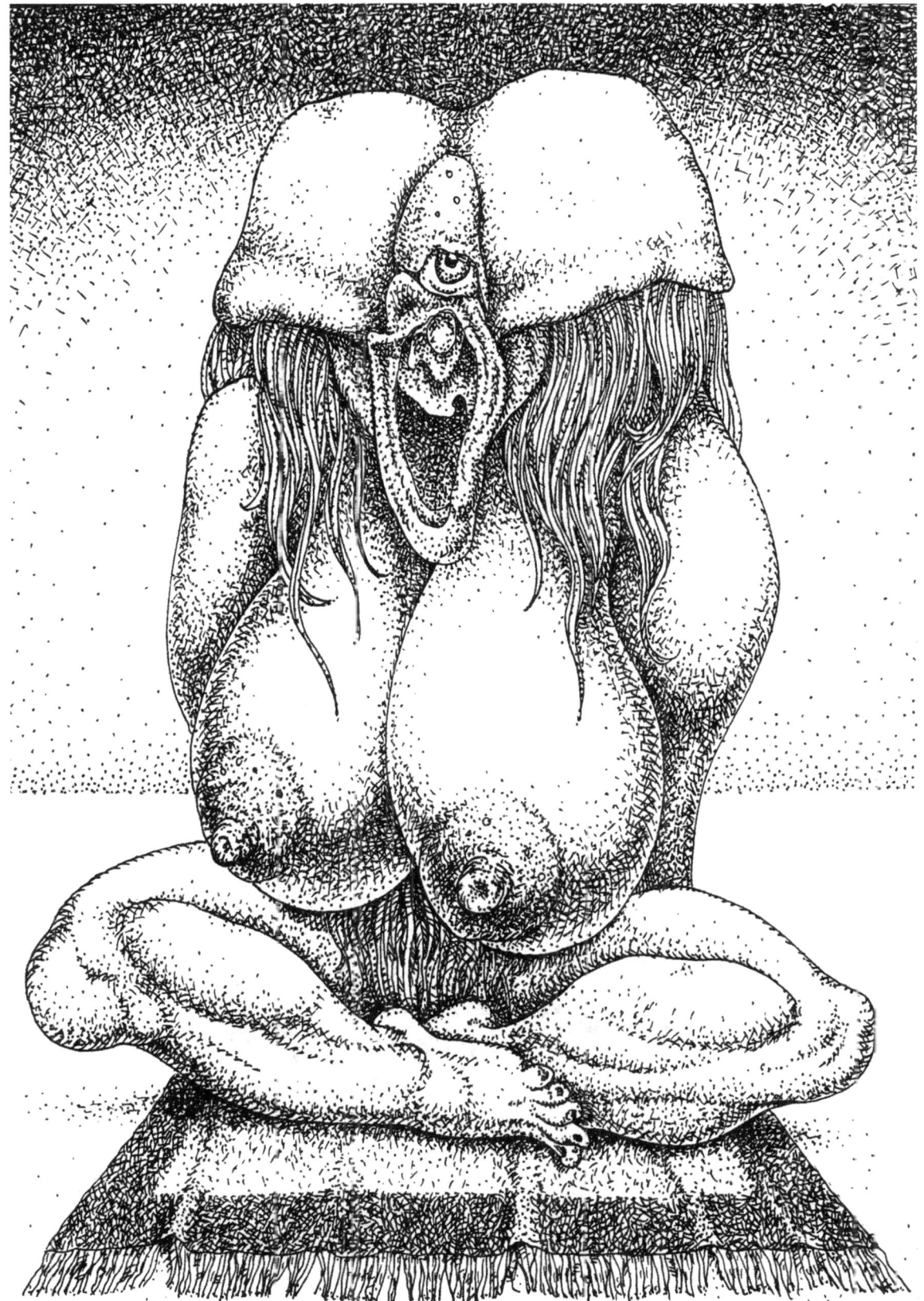

9

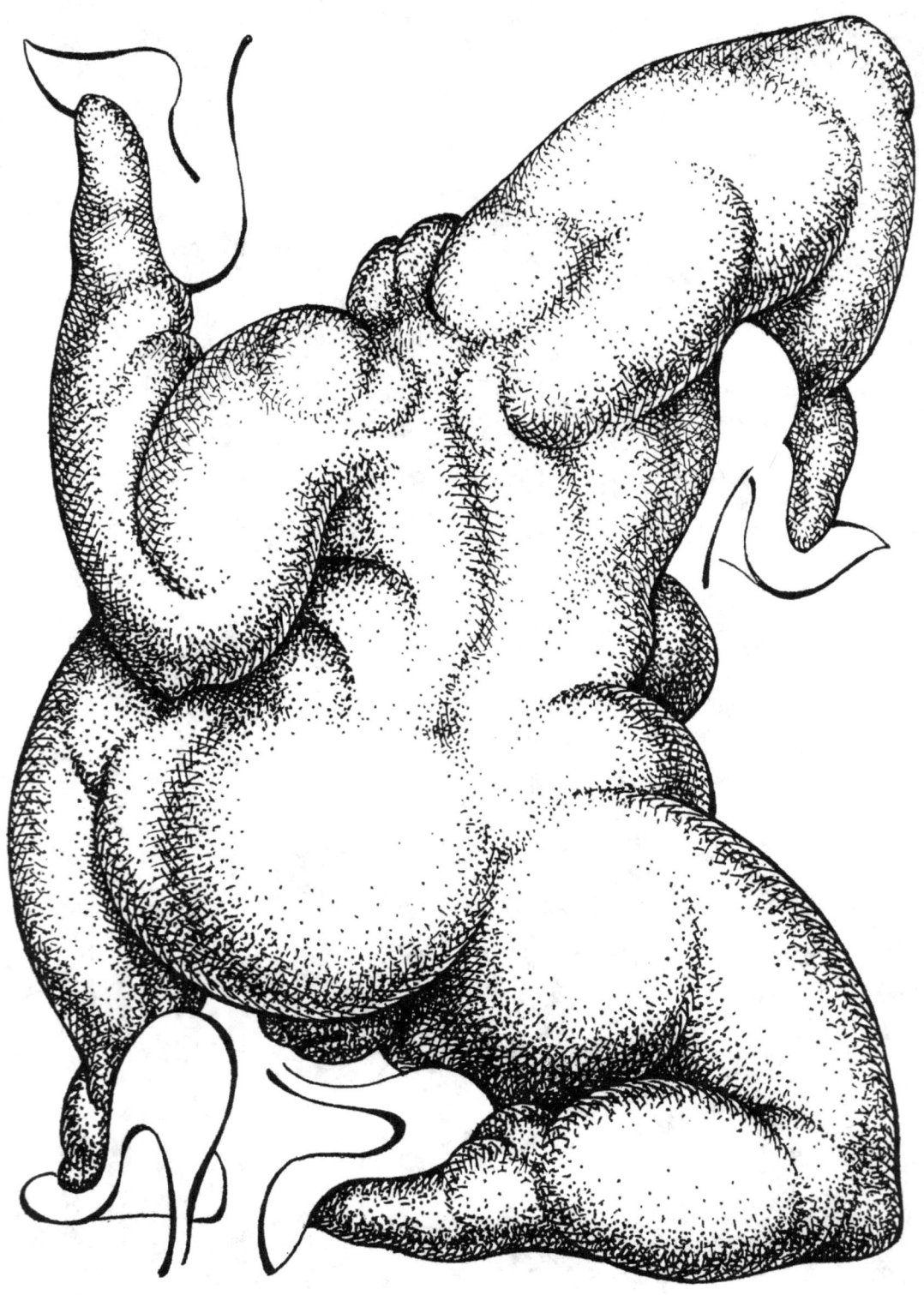

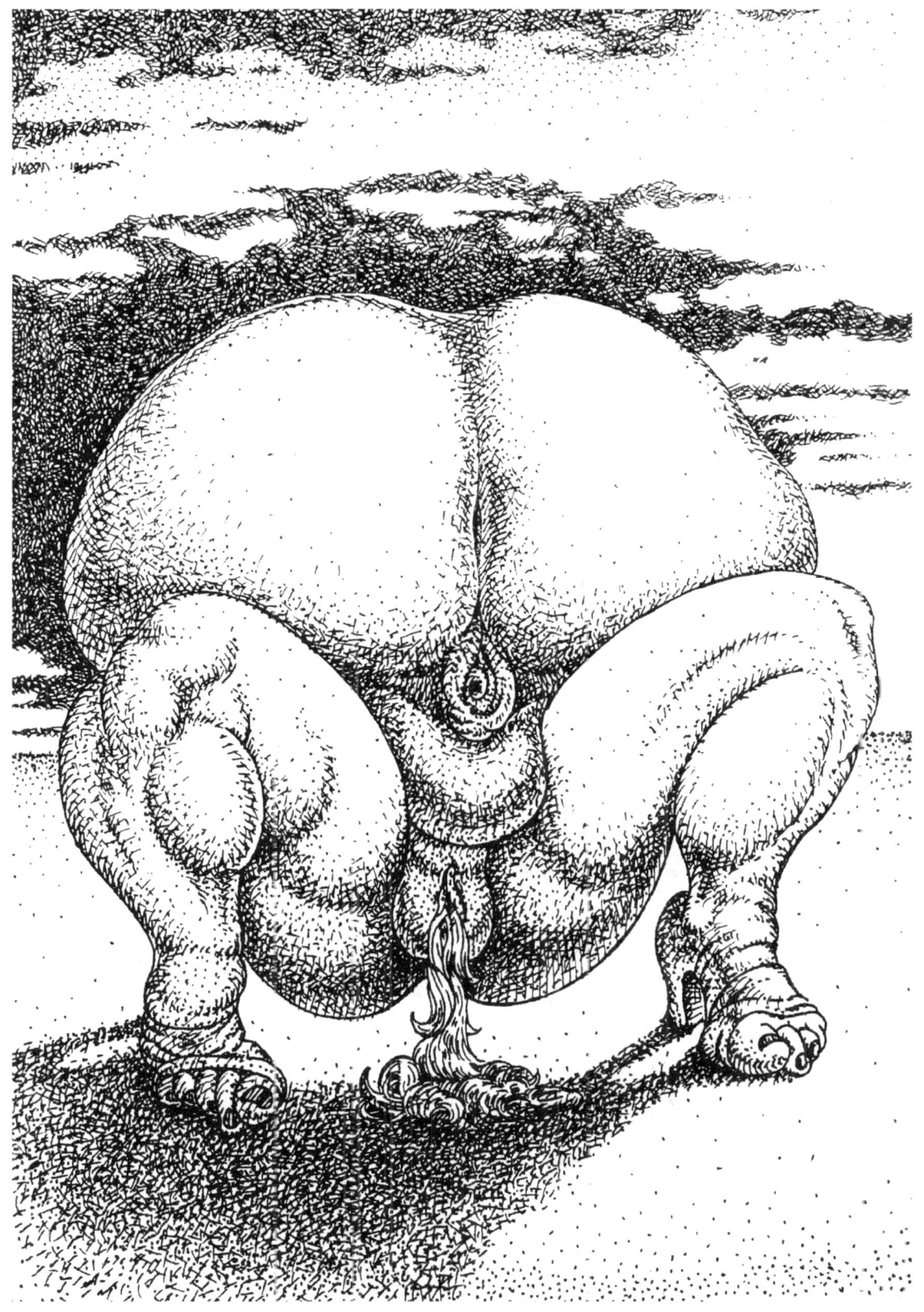

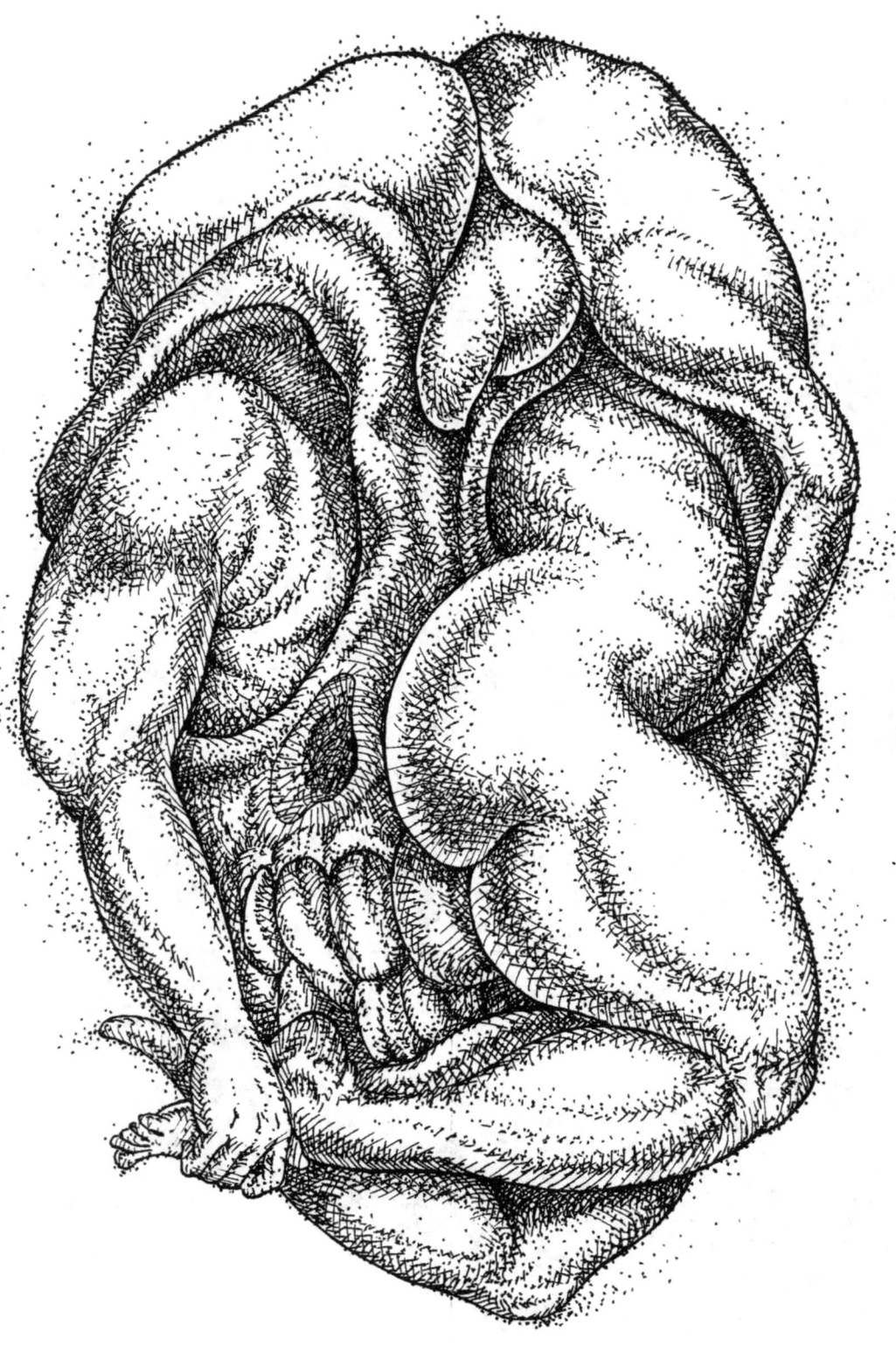

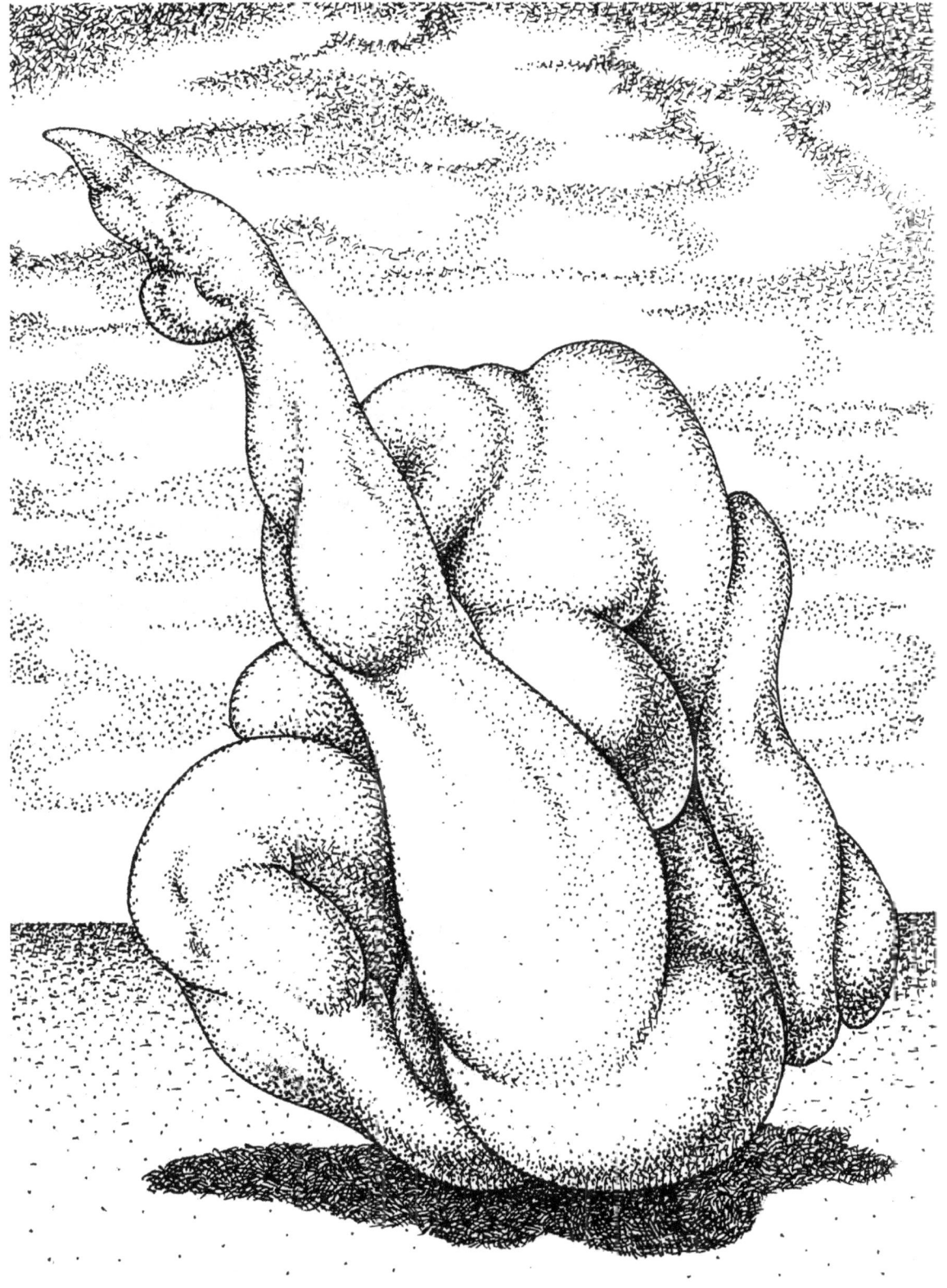

13

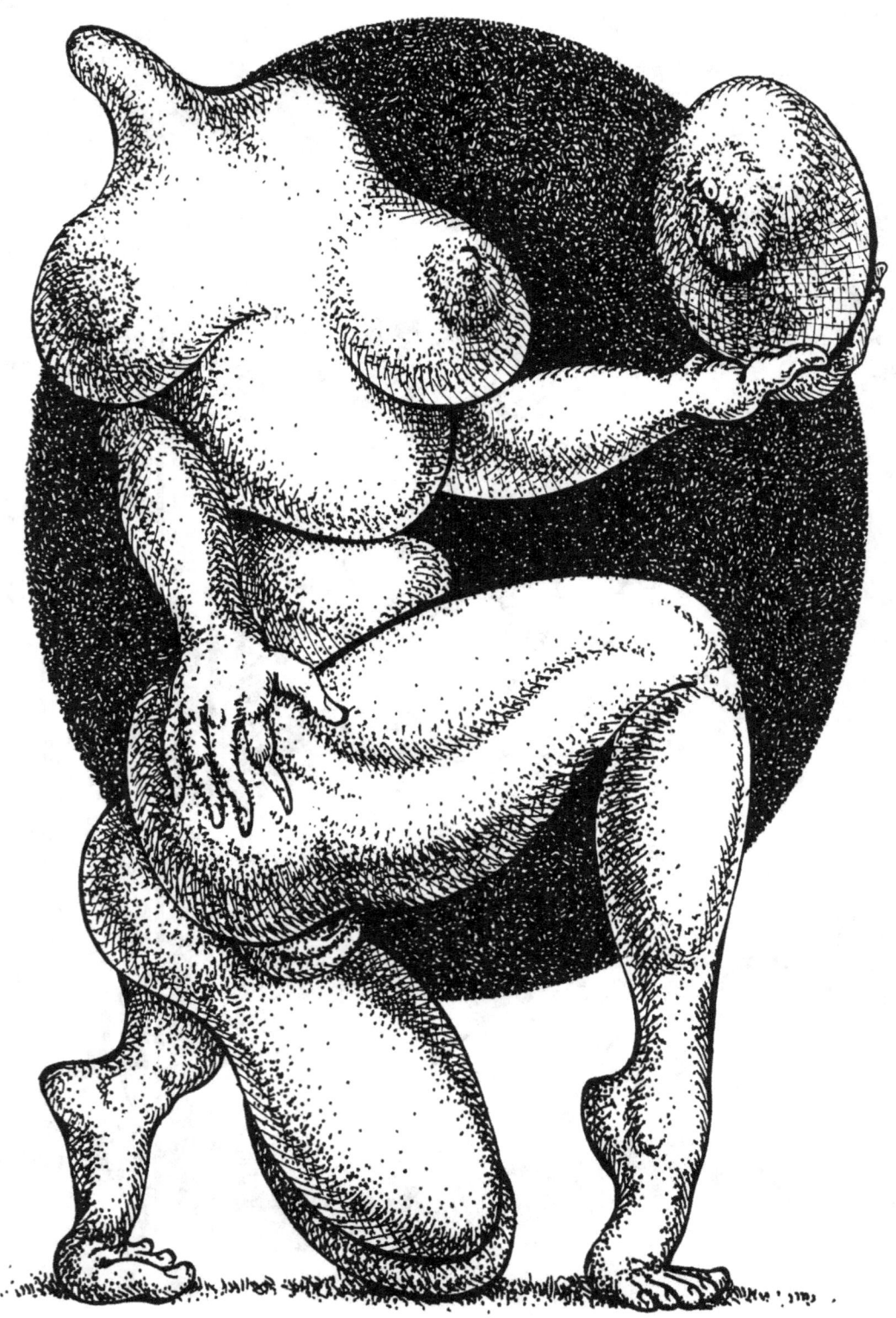

14

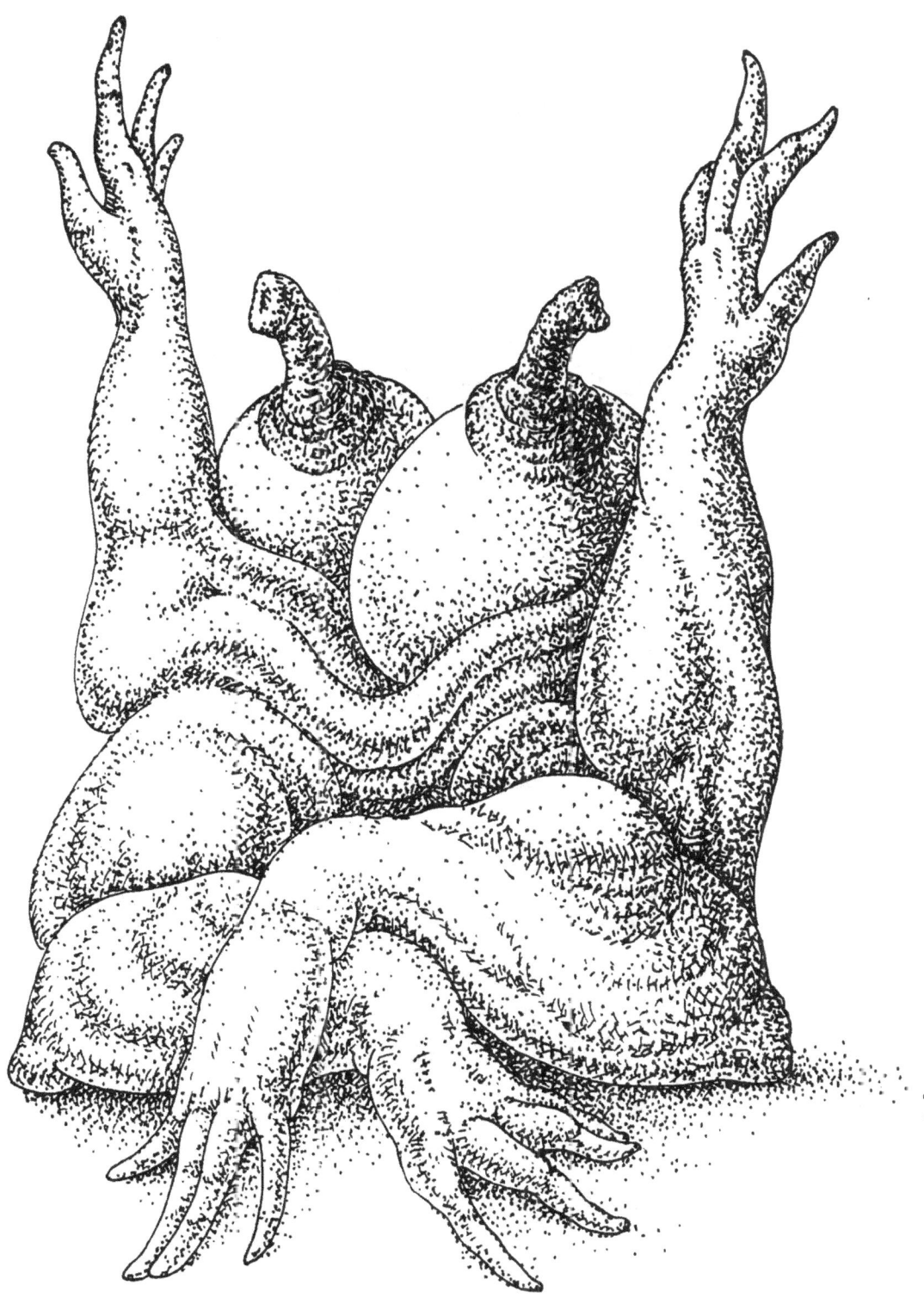

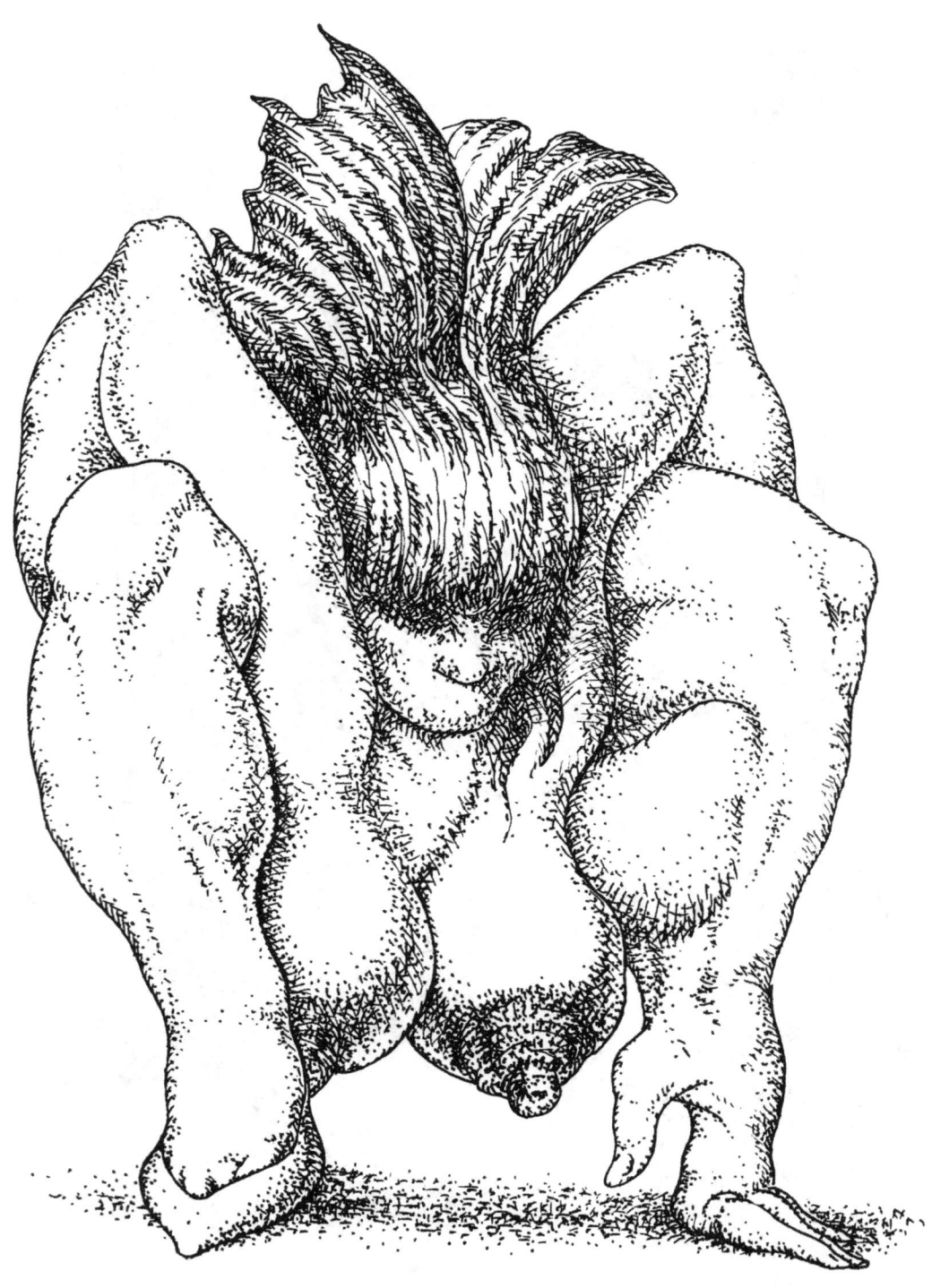

16

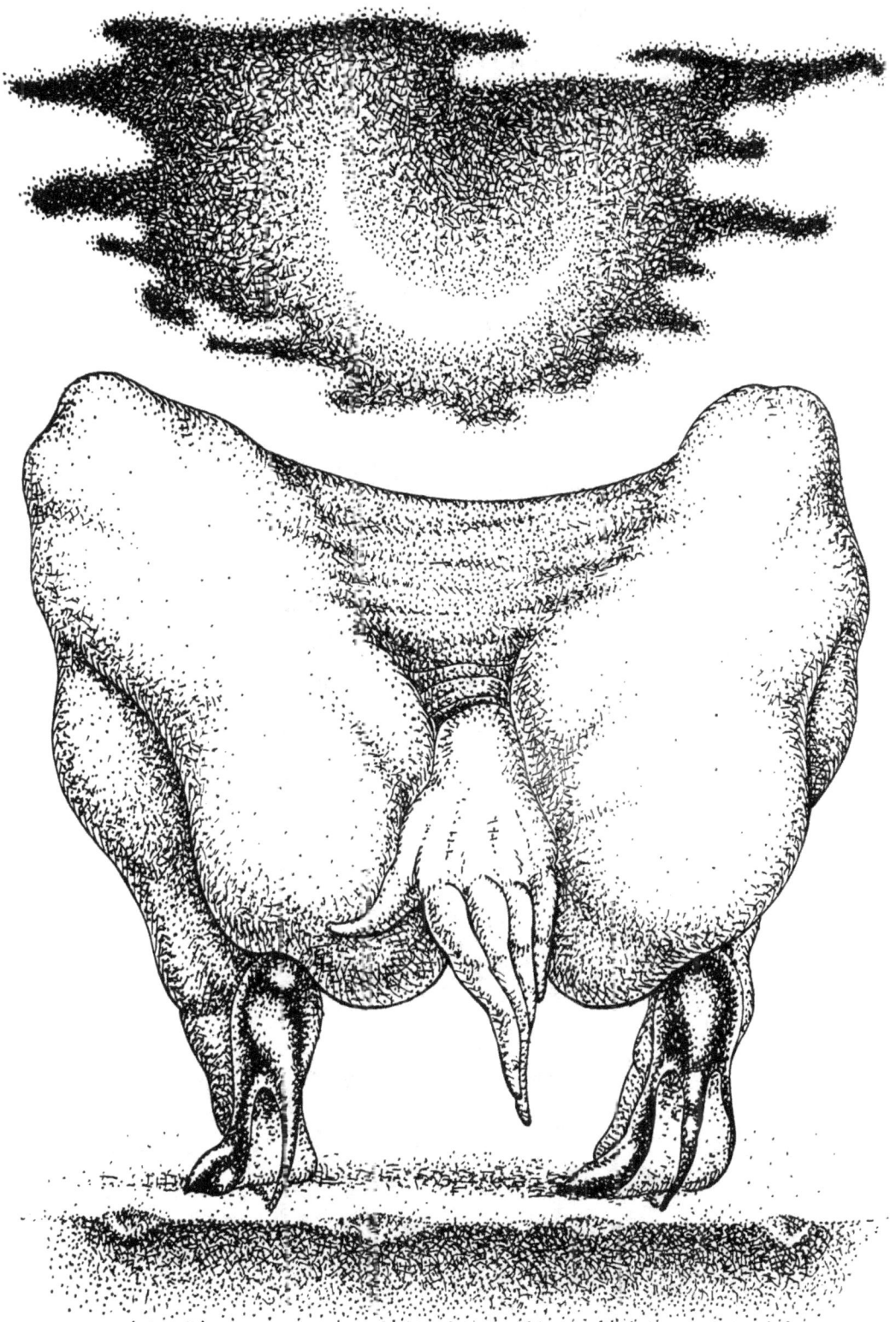

17

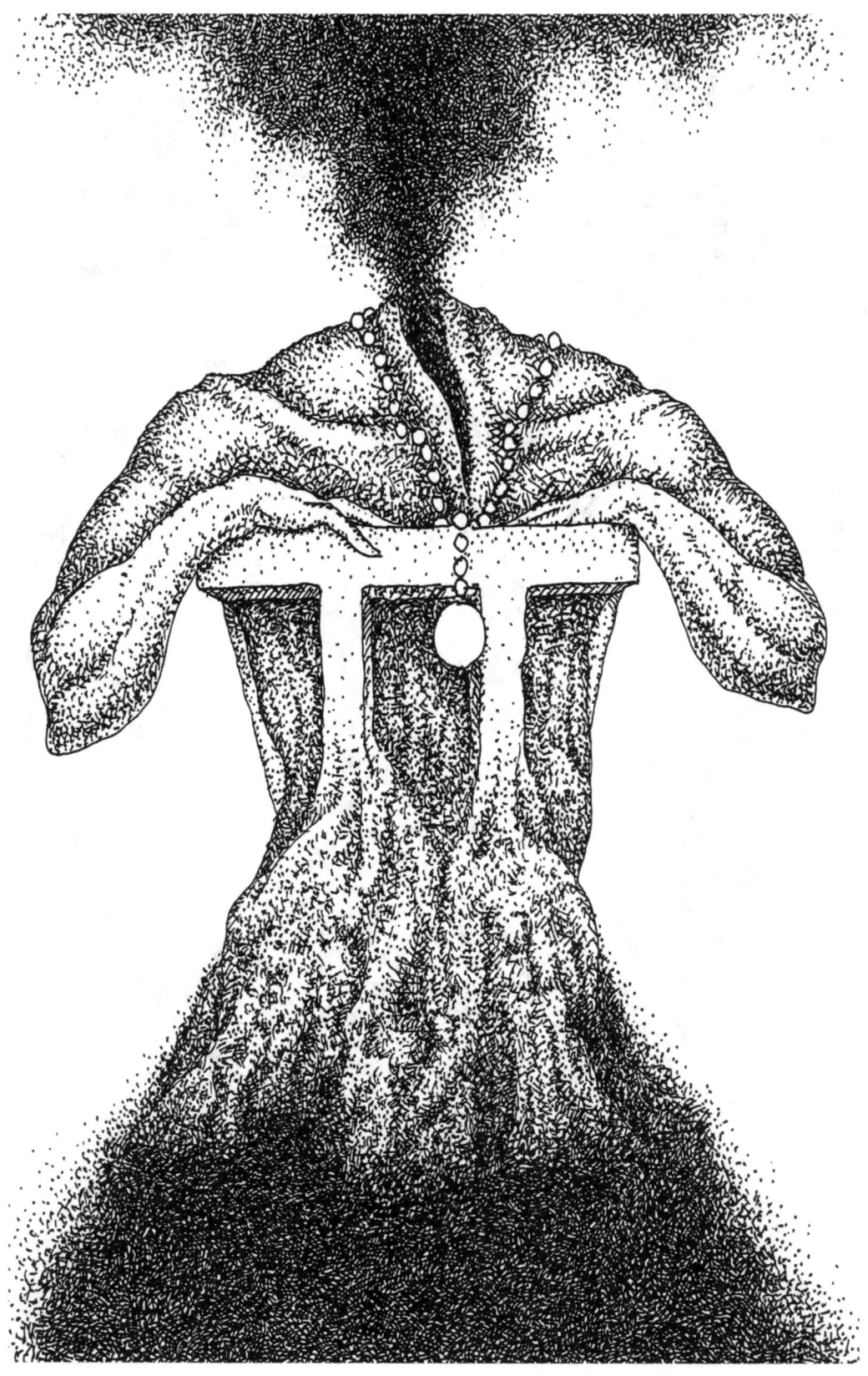

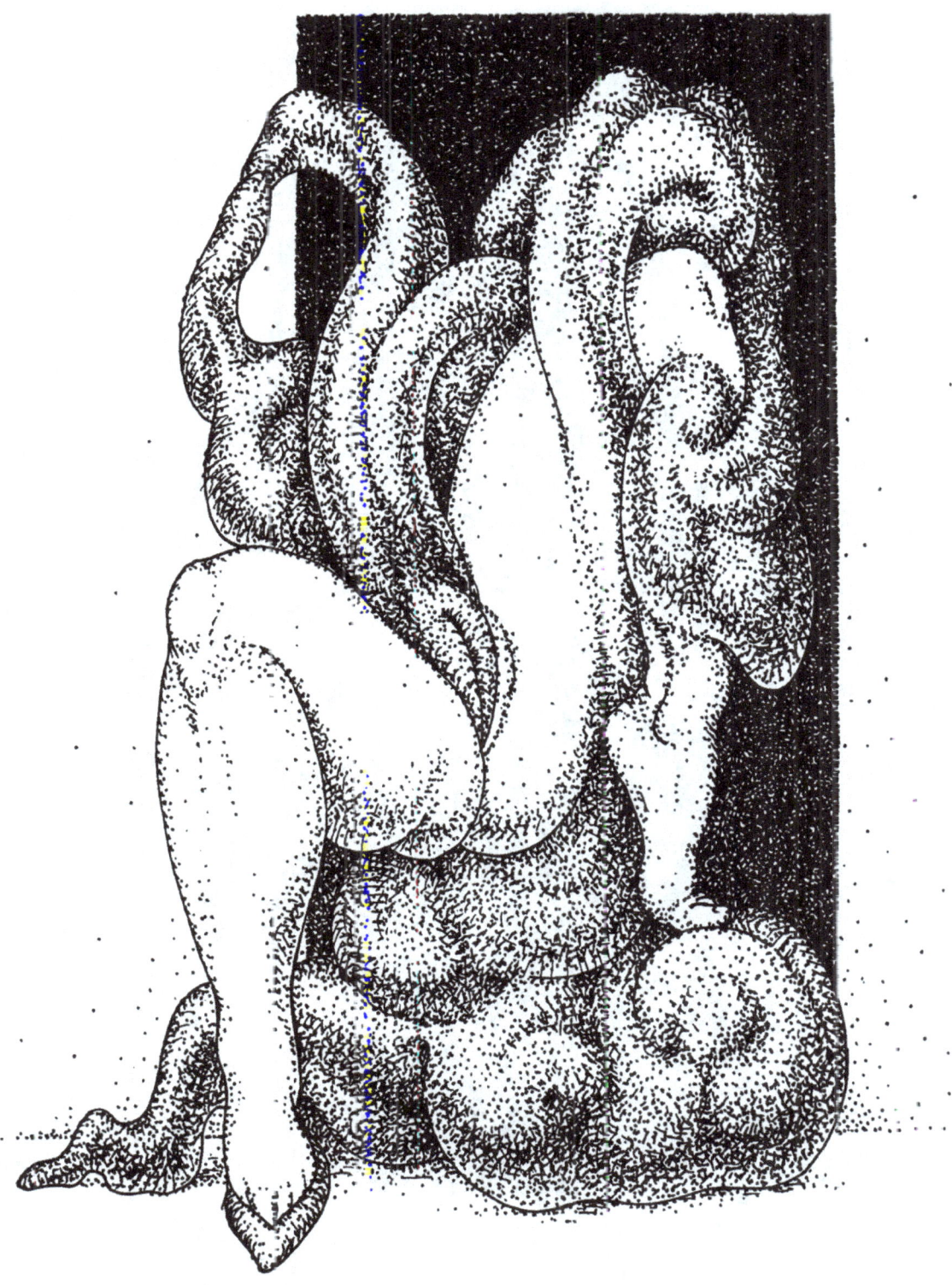

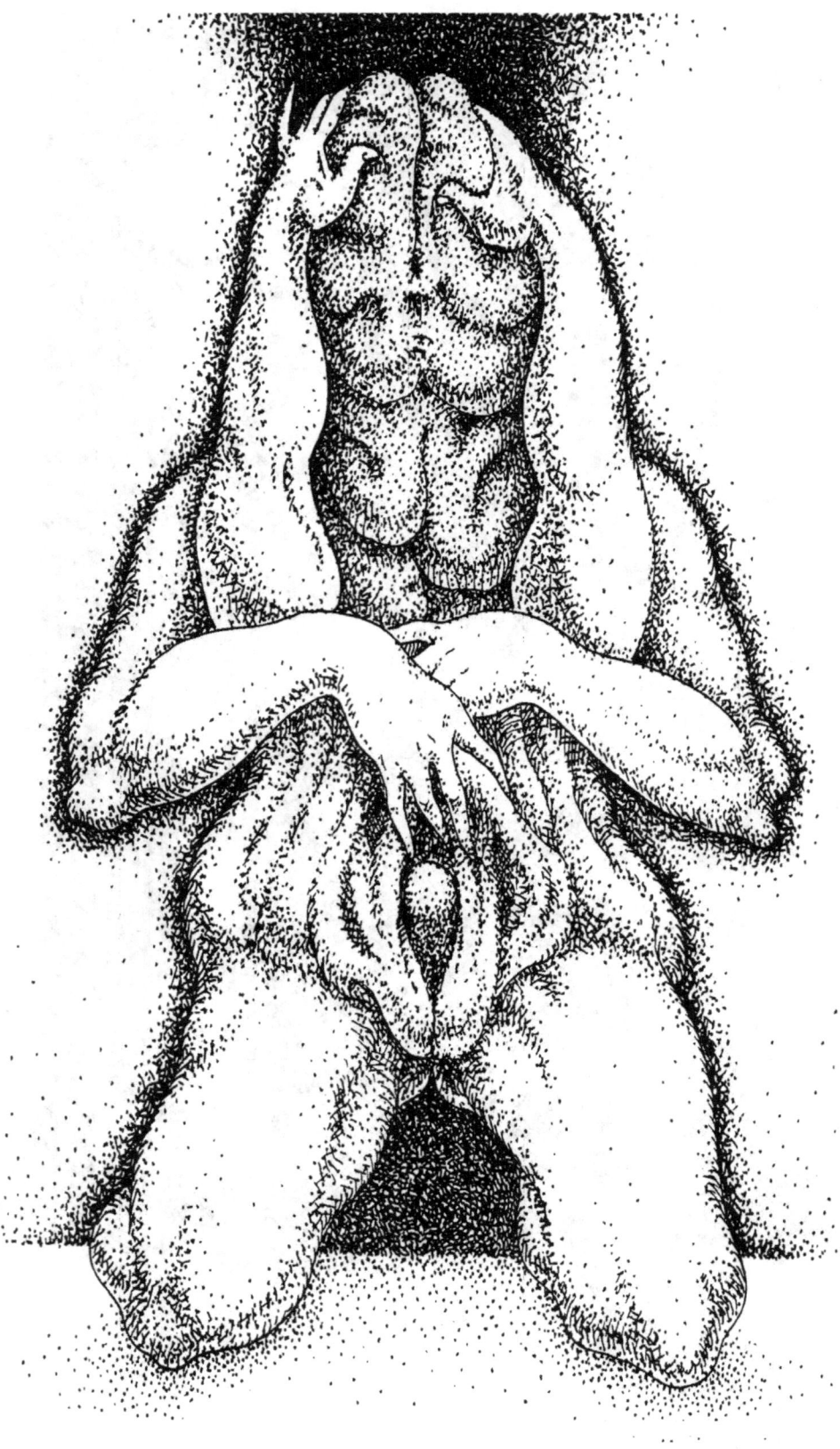

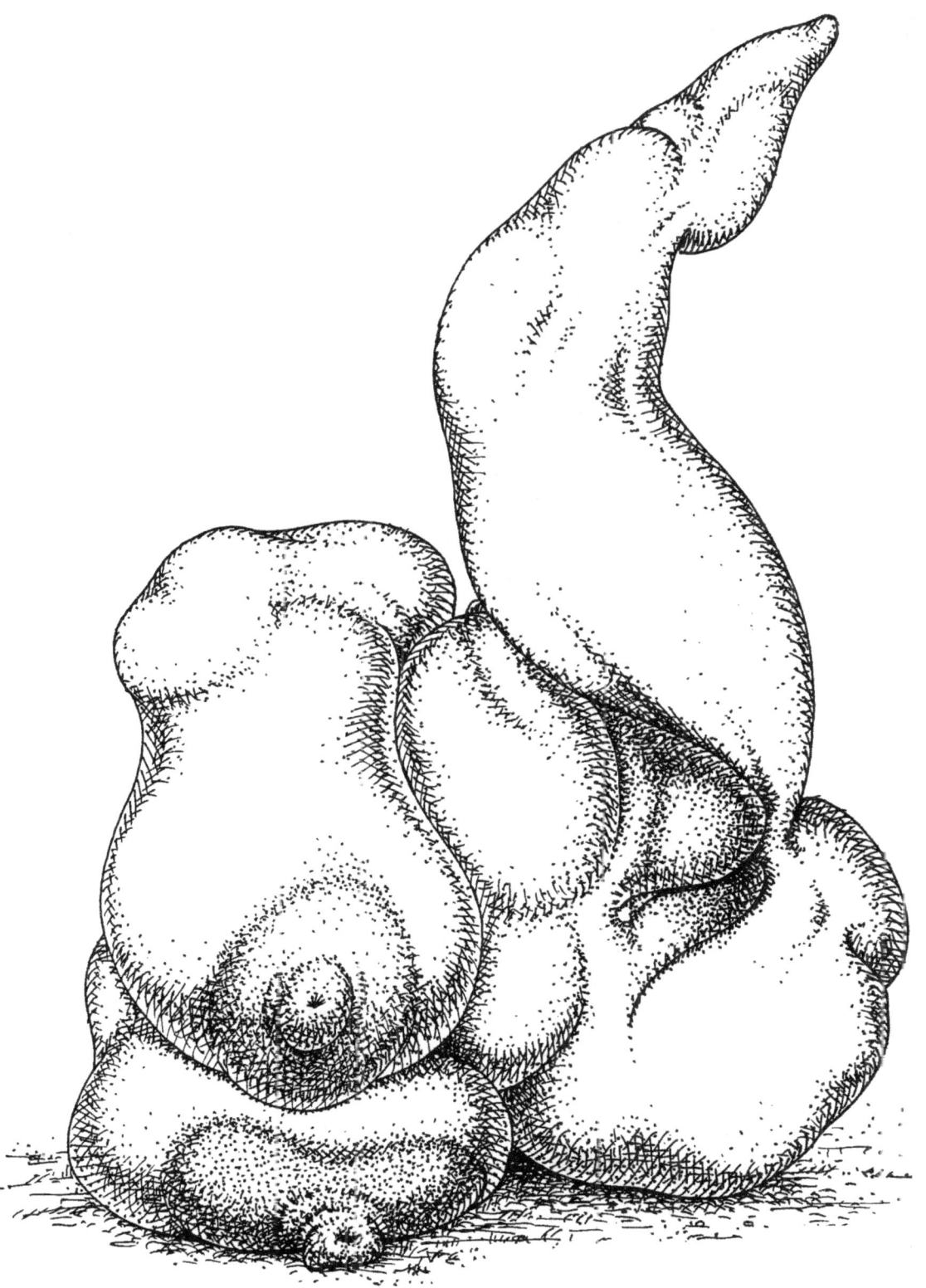

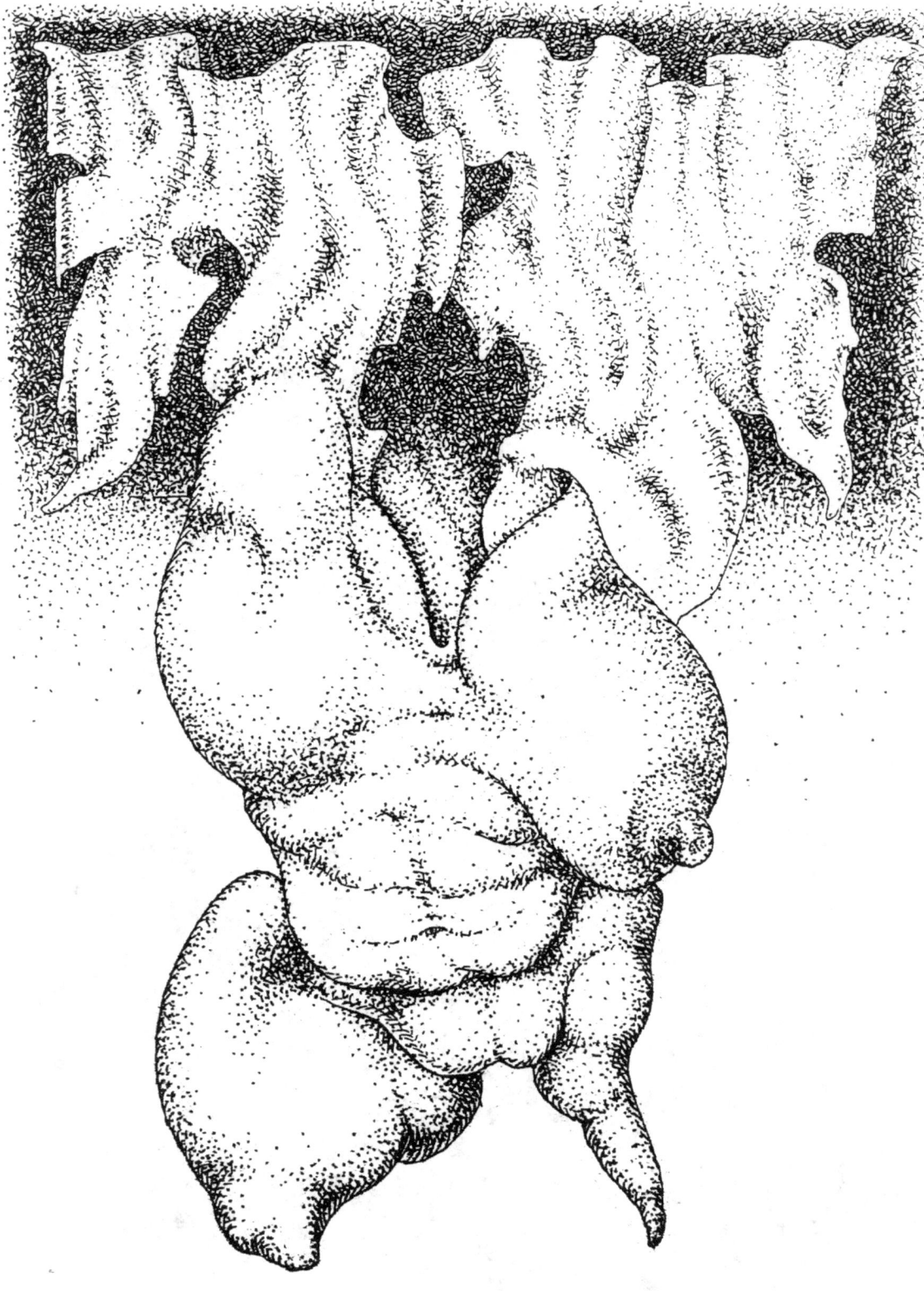

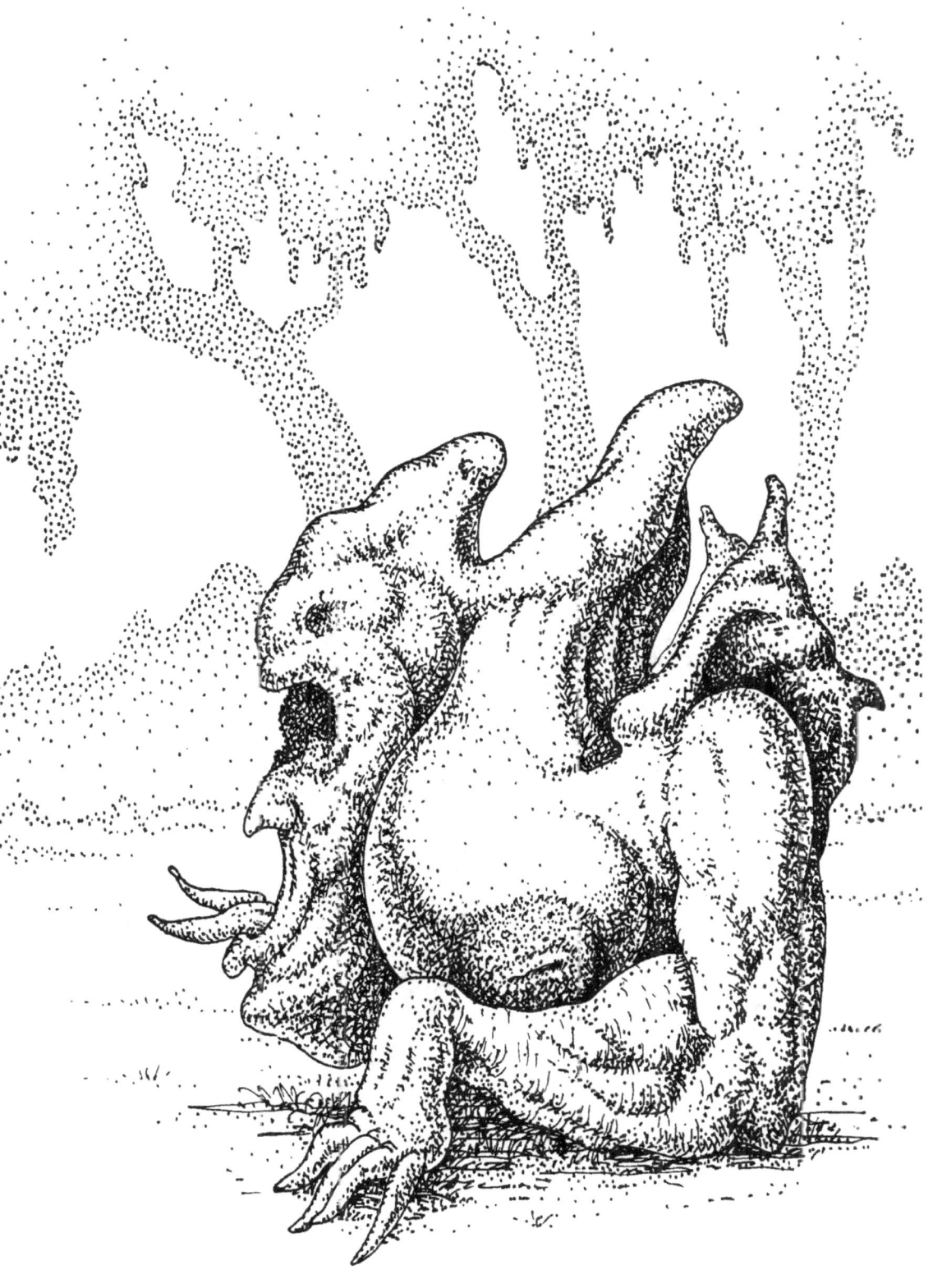

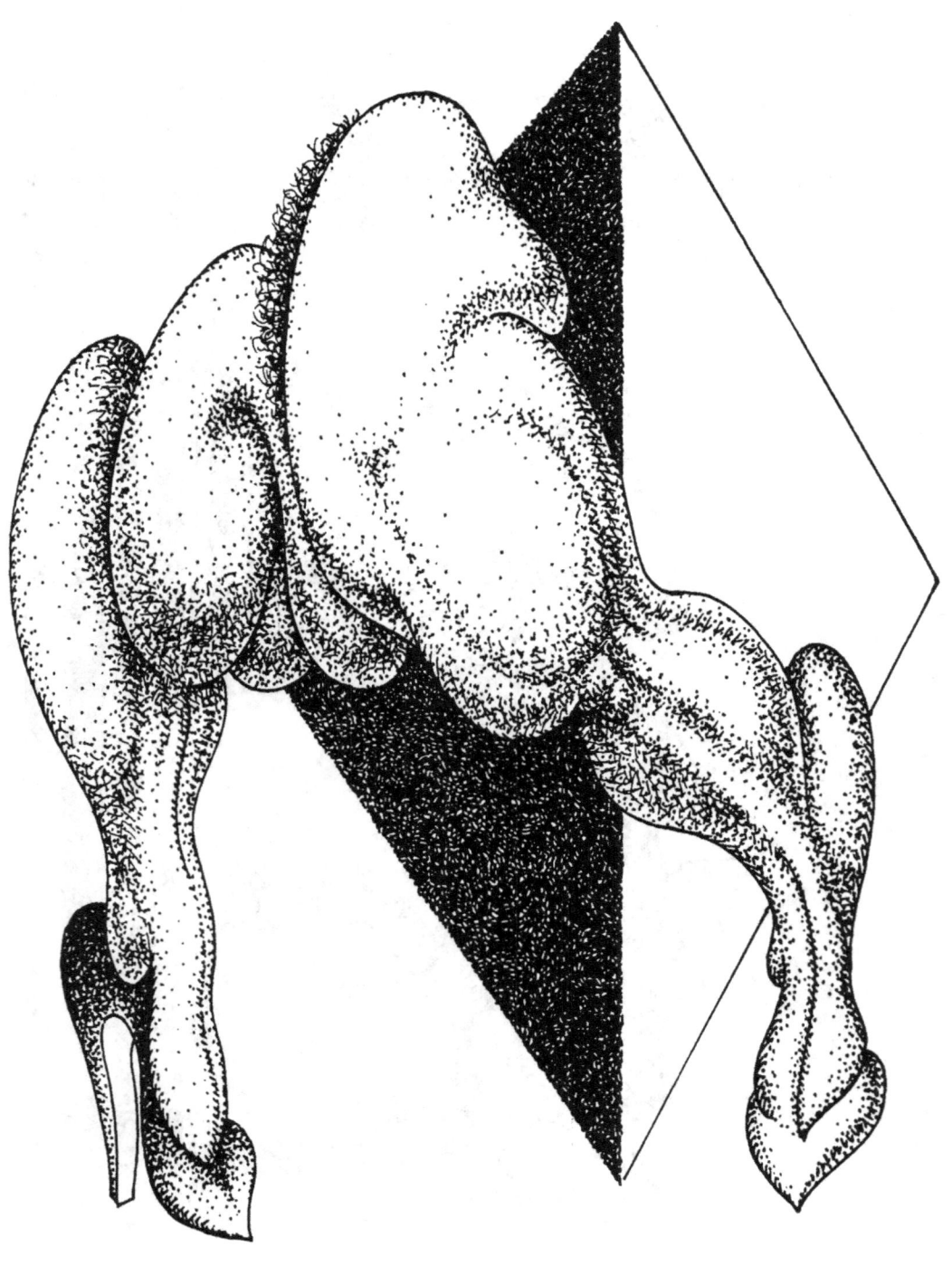

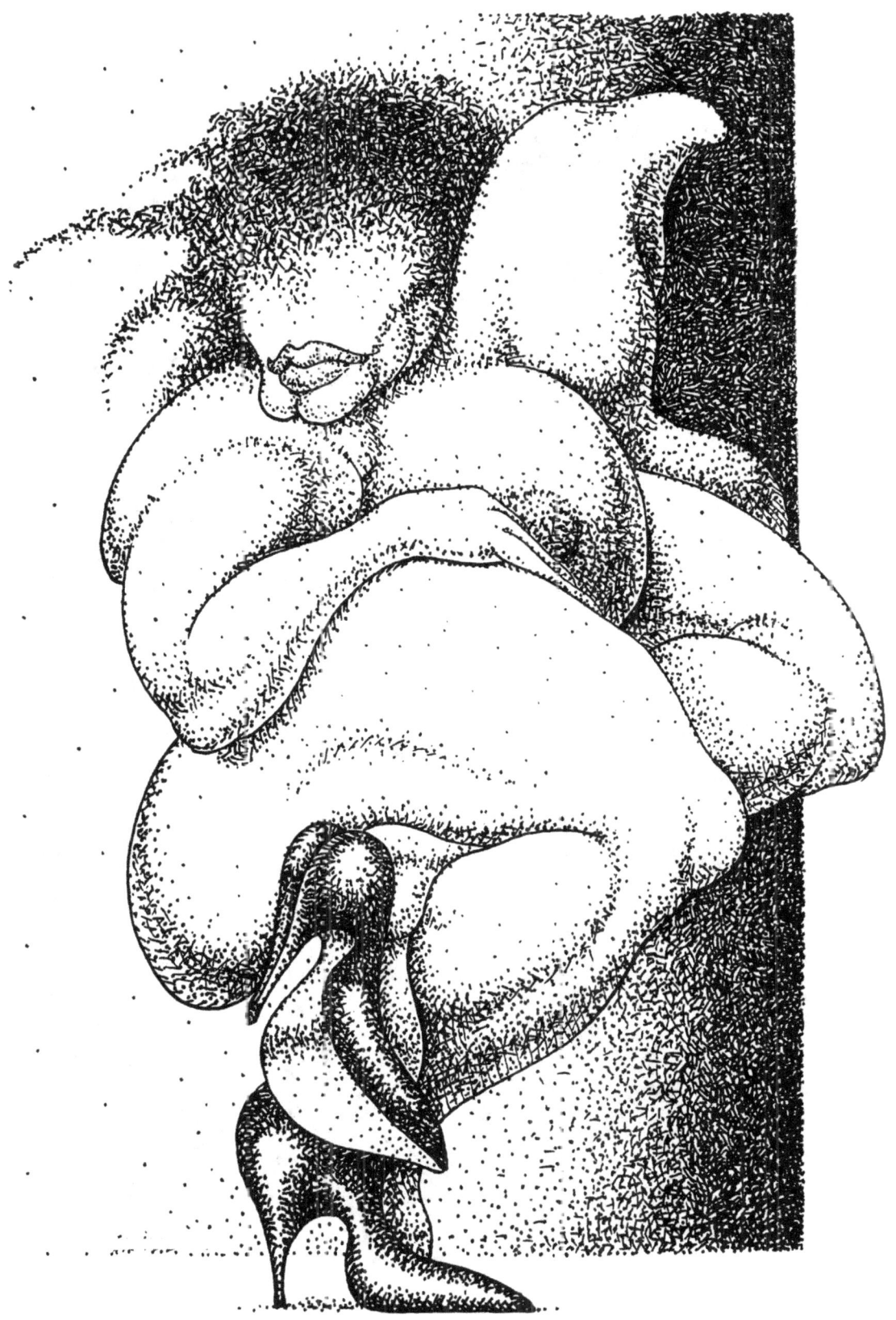

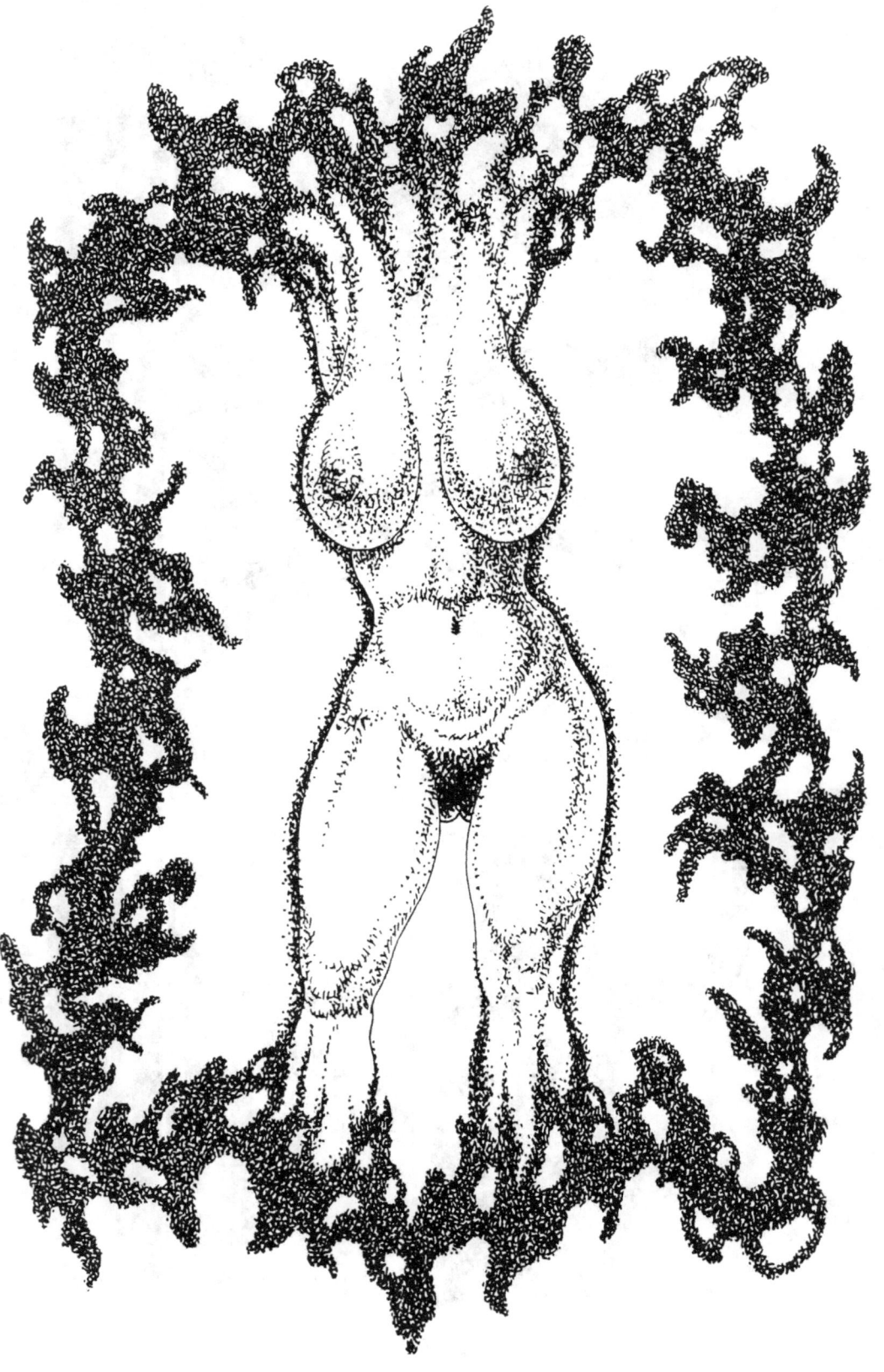

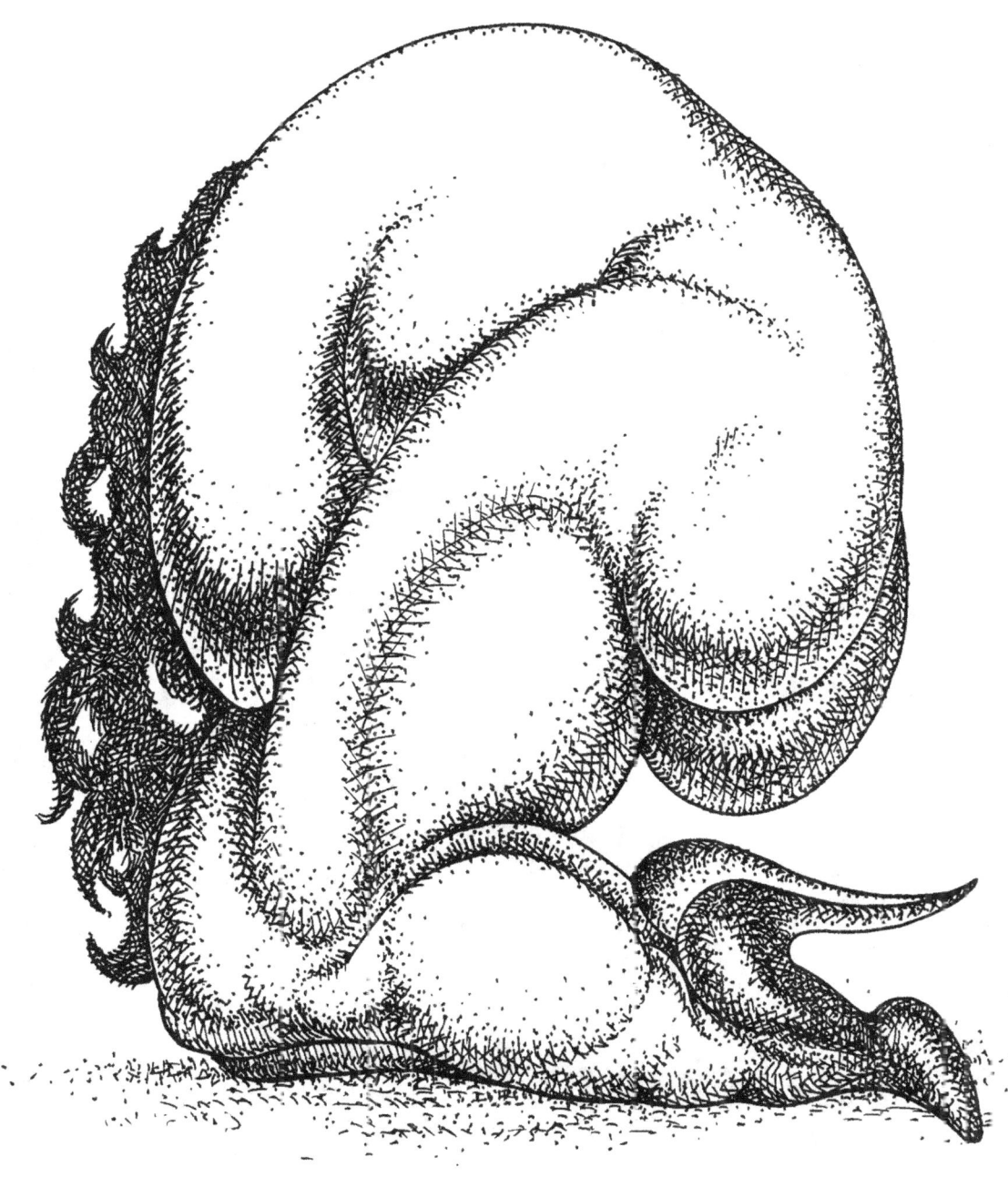

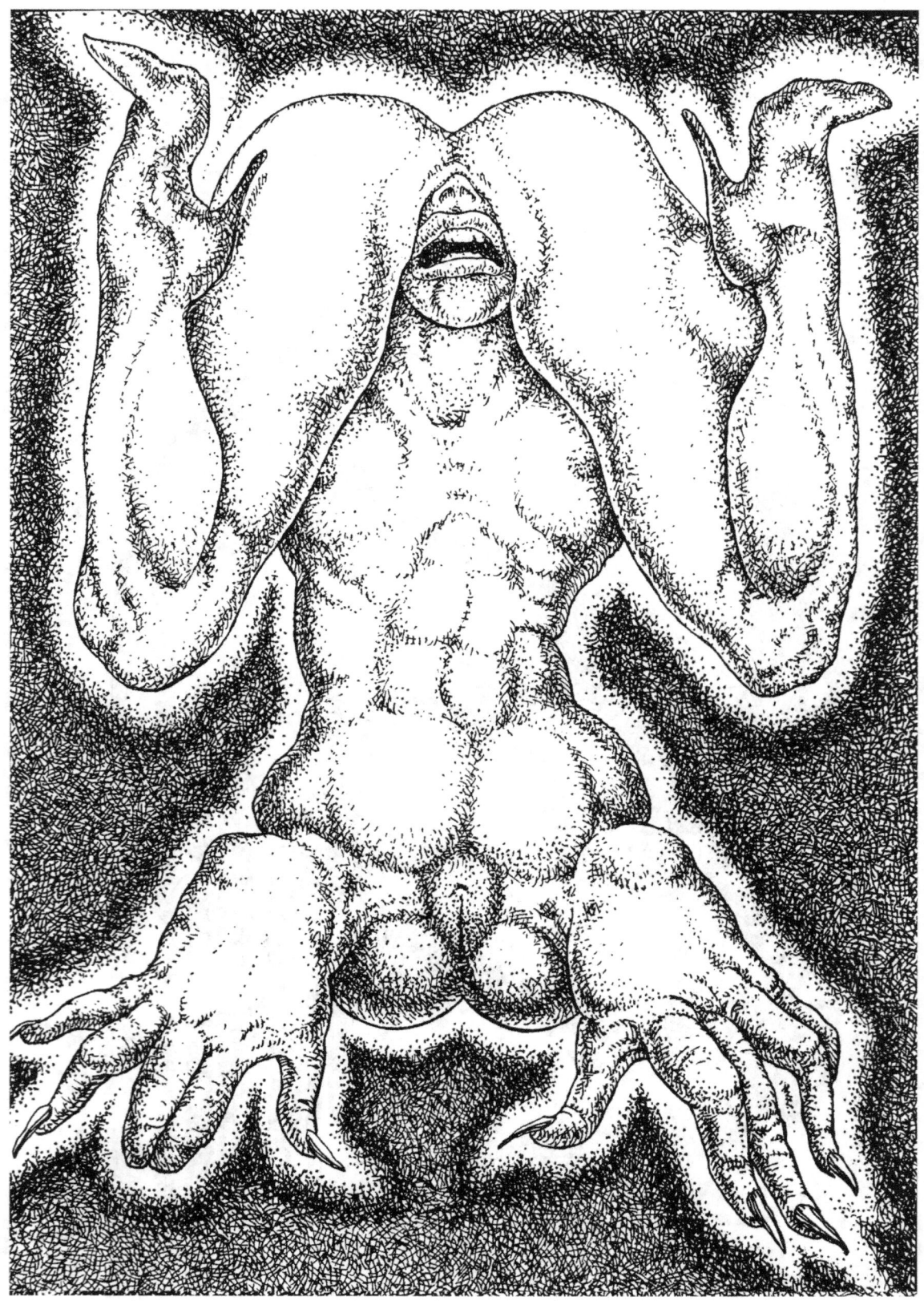

28

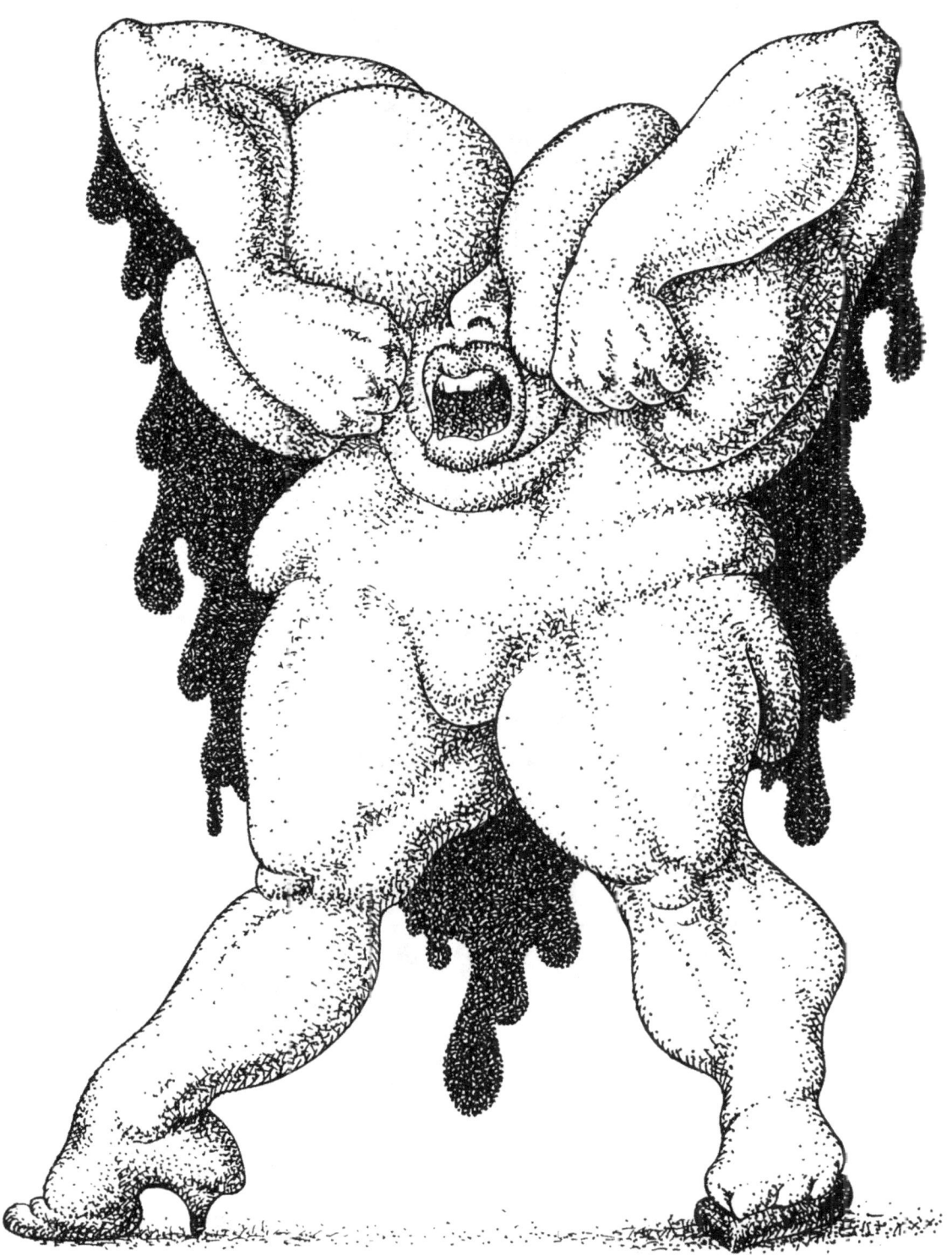

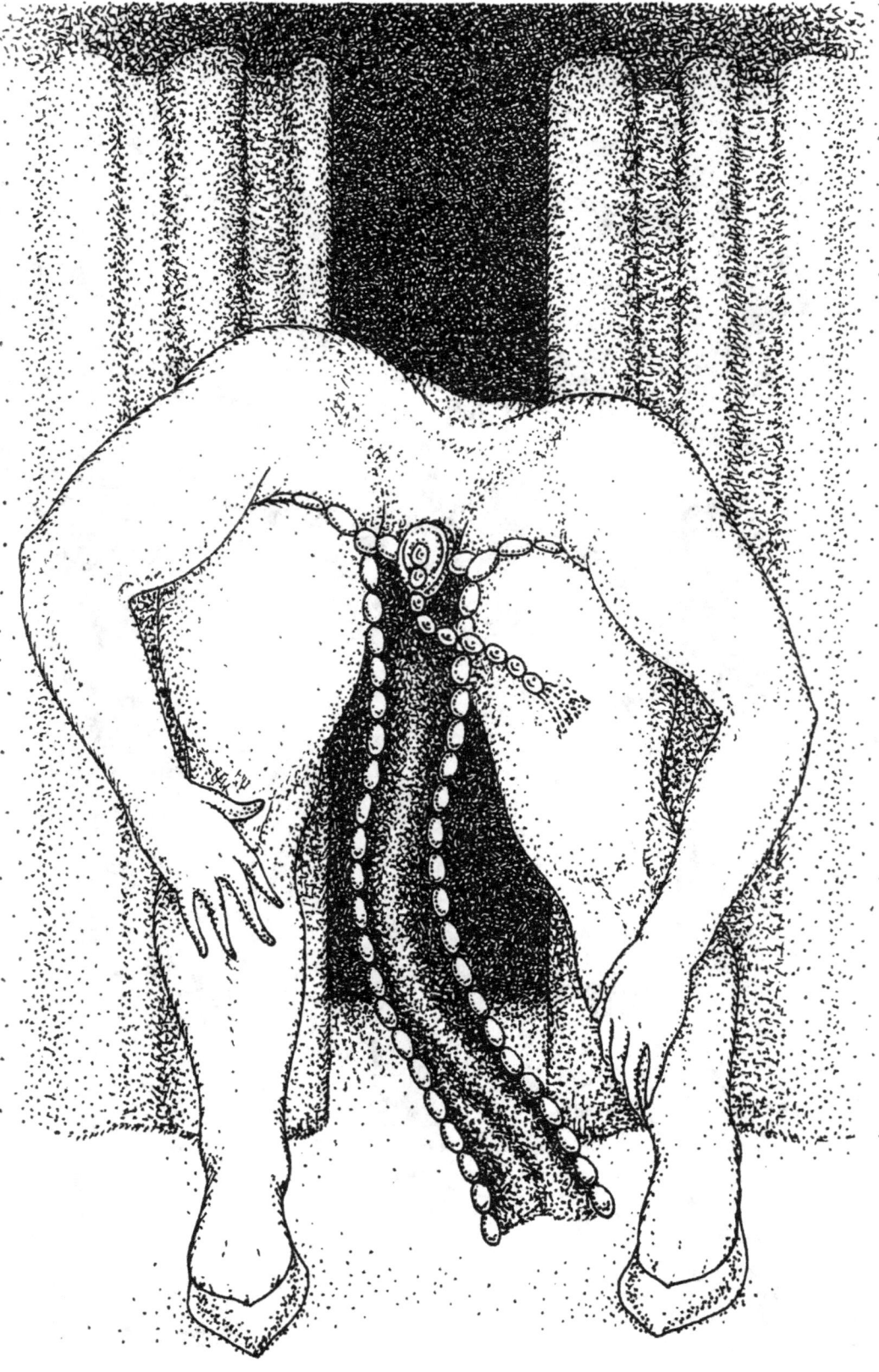

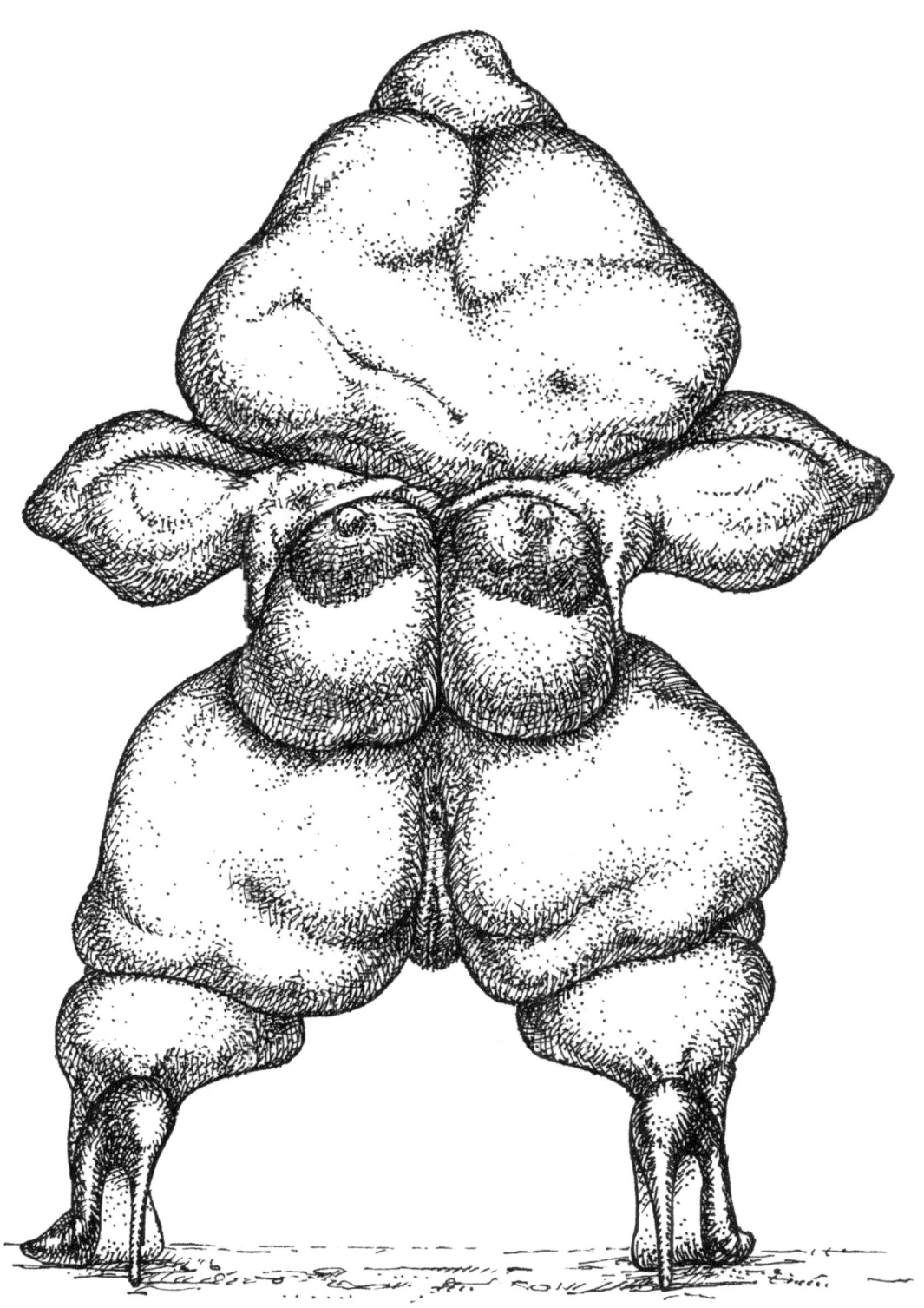

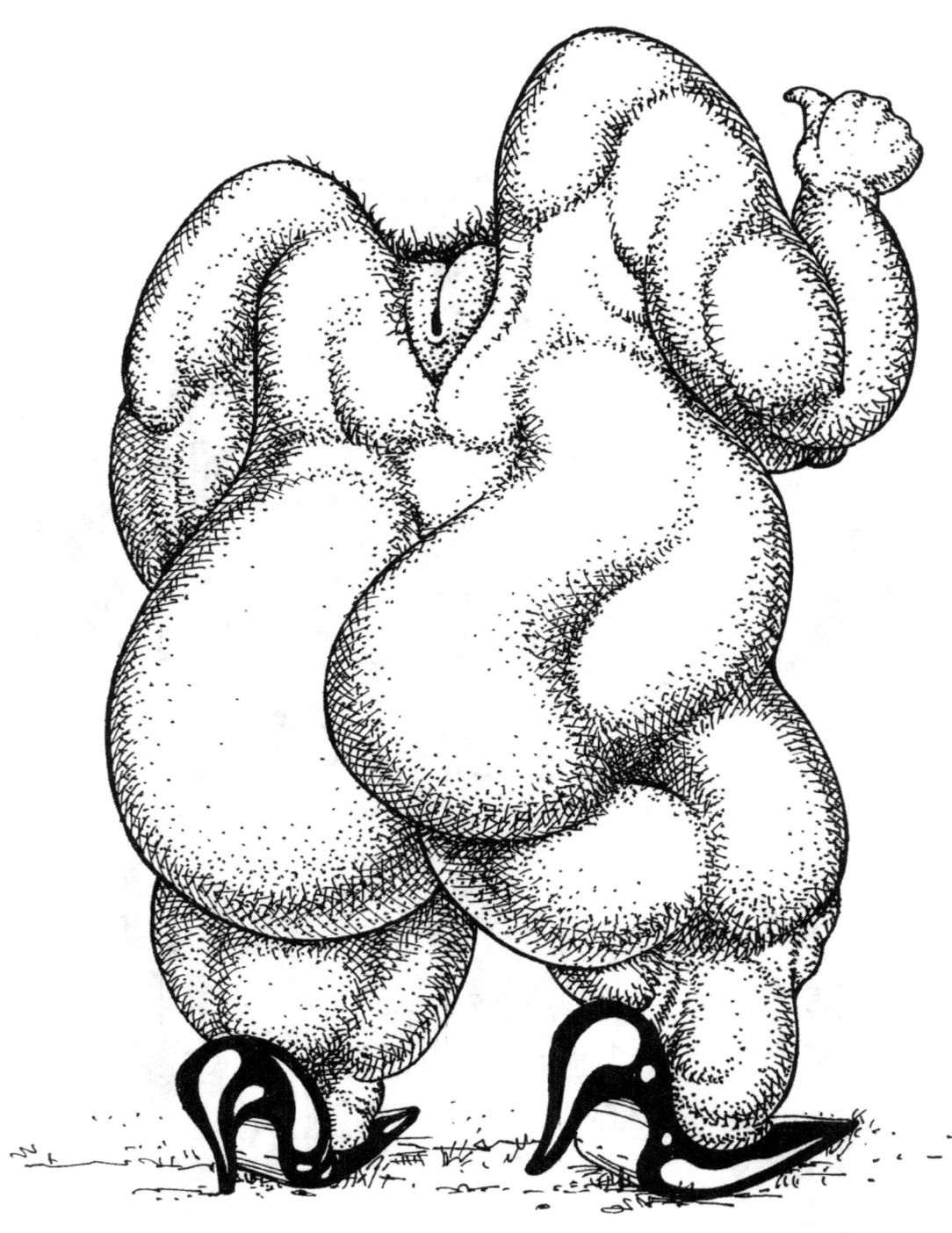

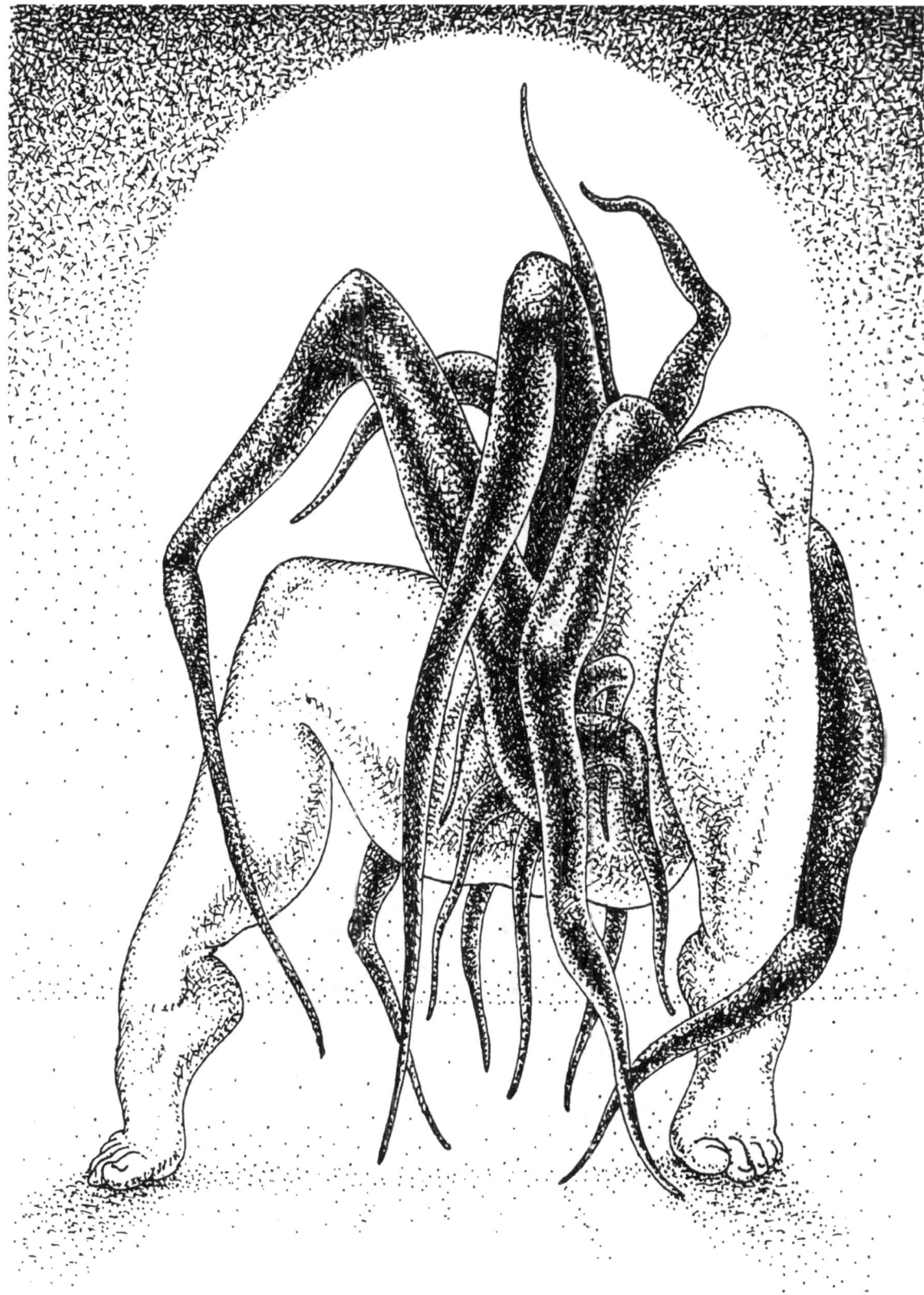

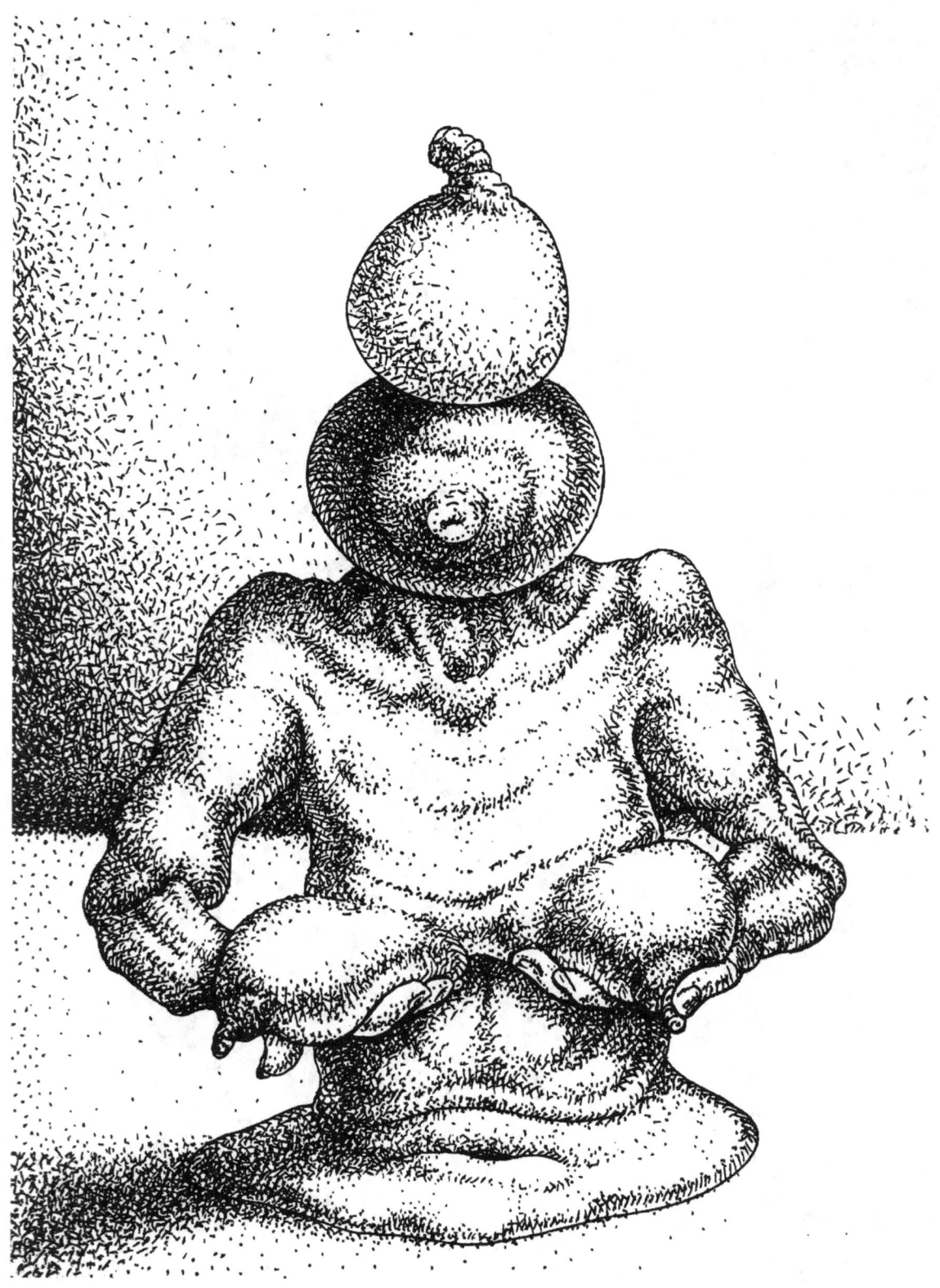

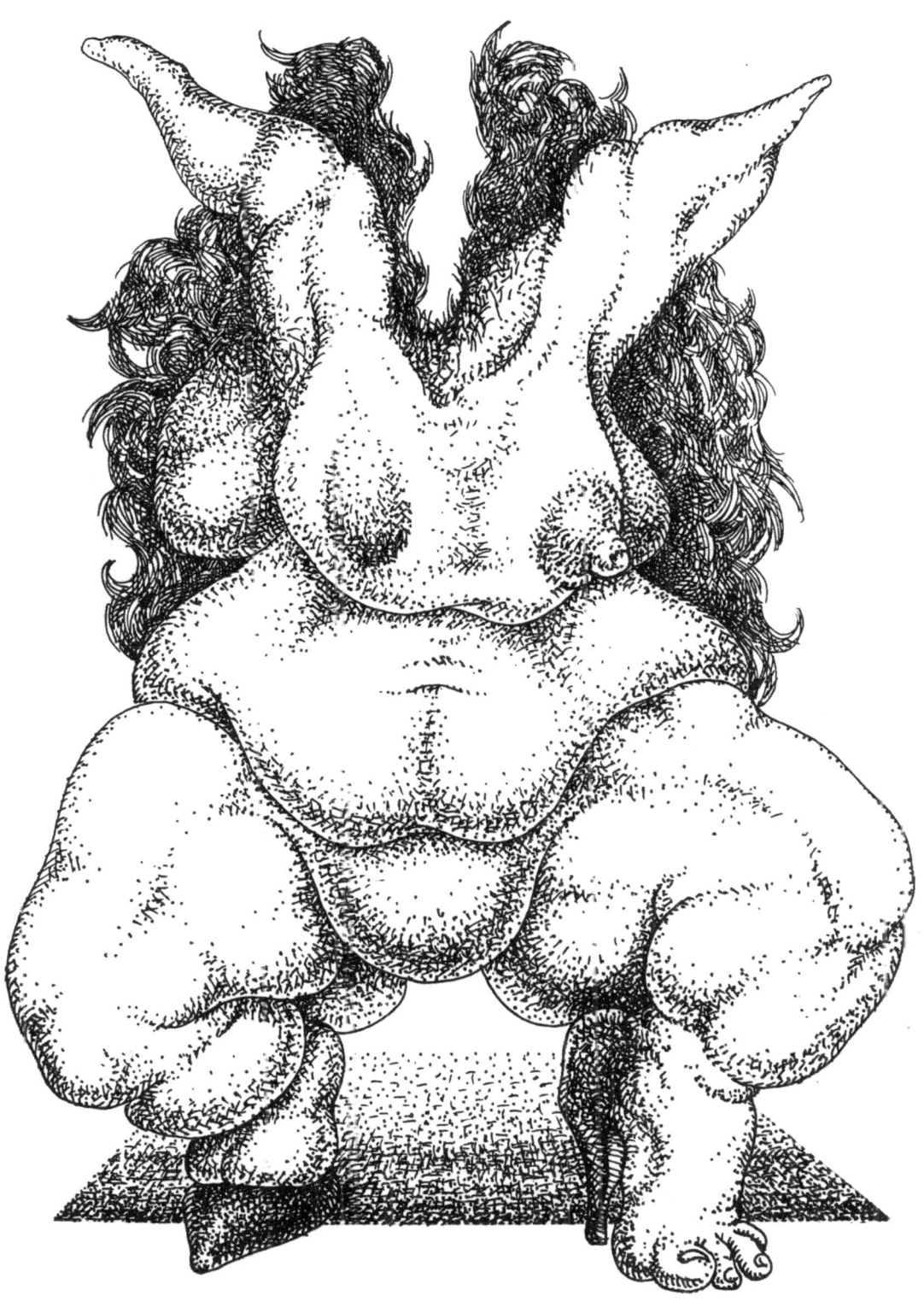

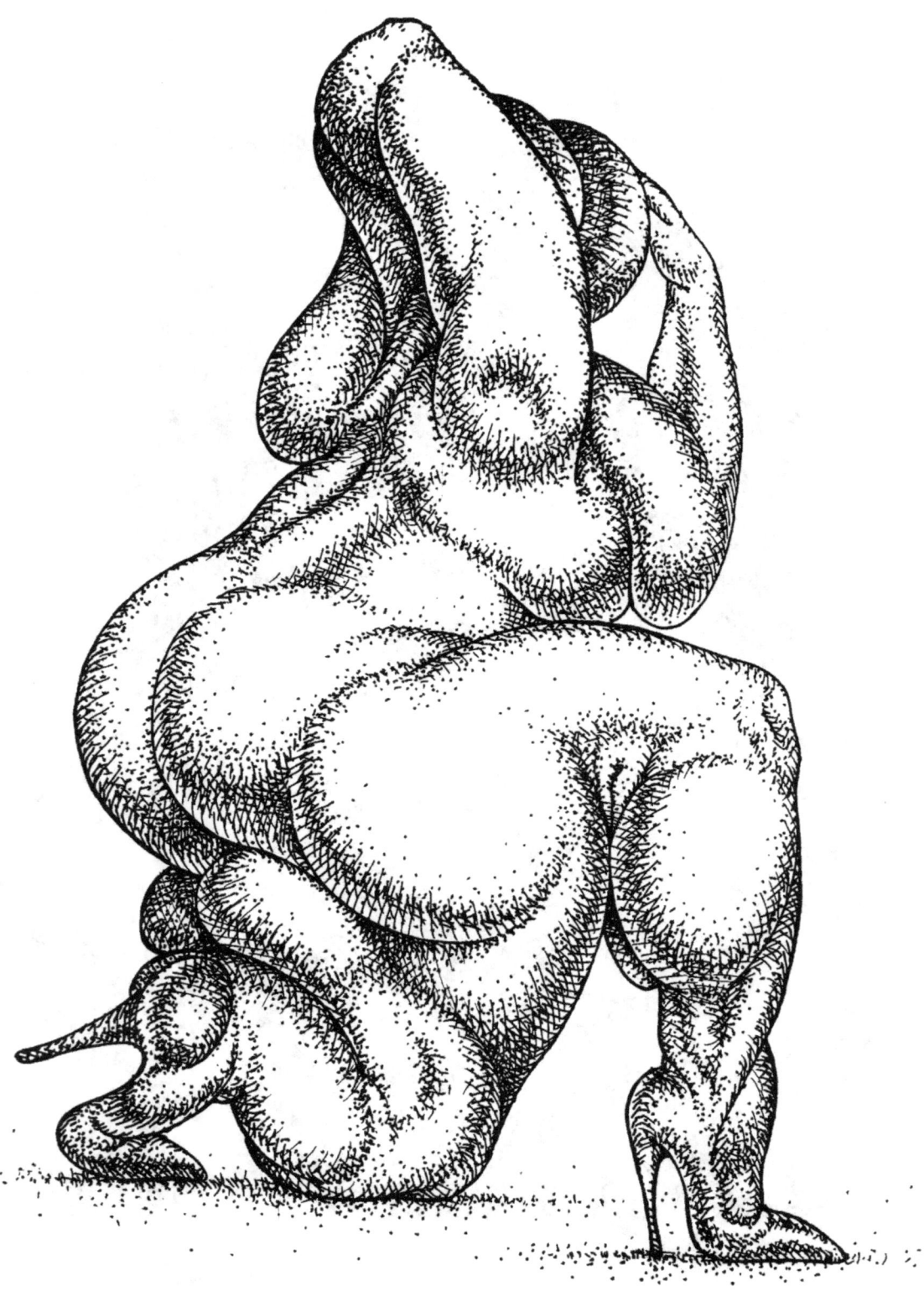

36

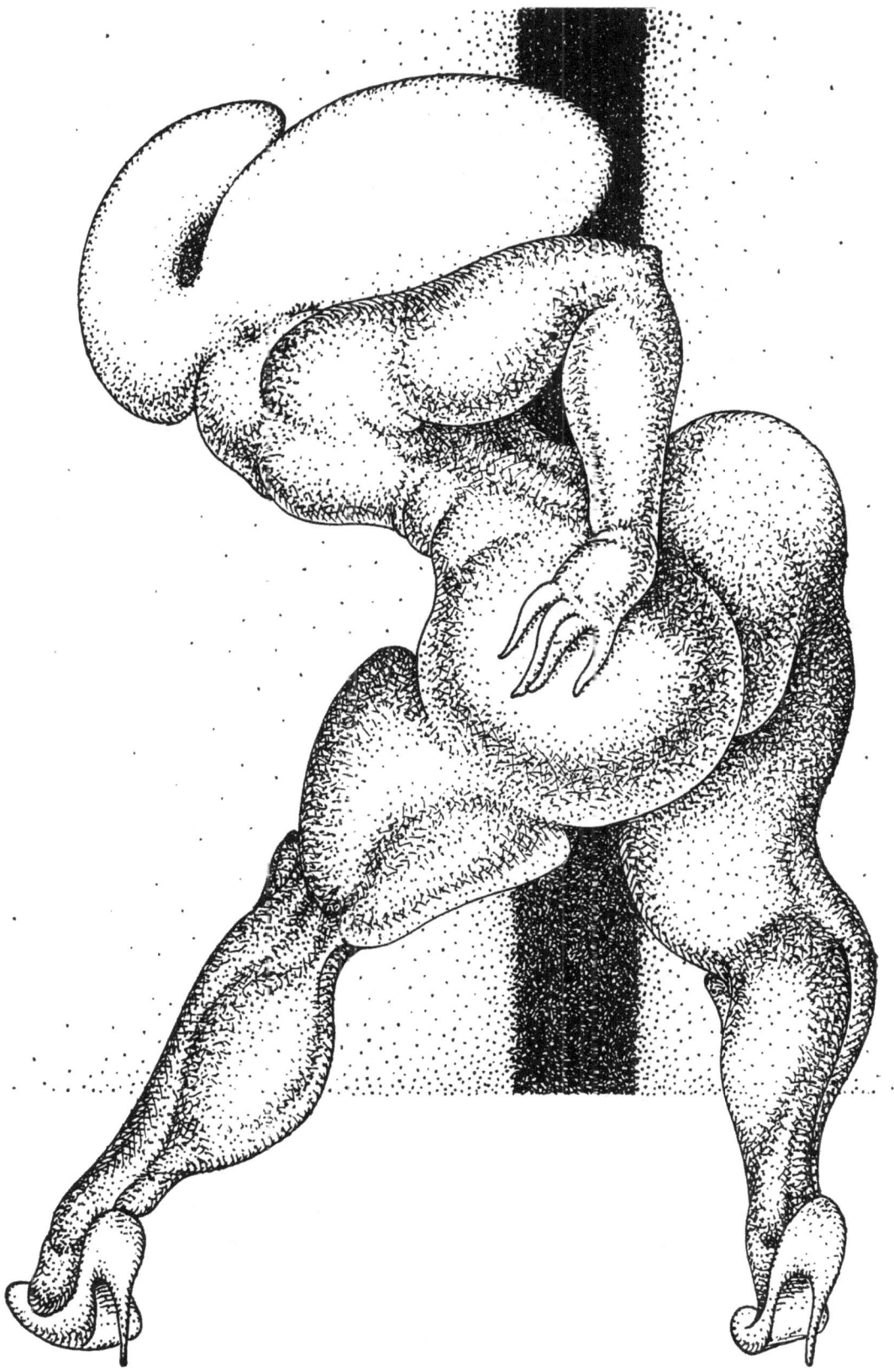

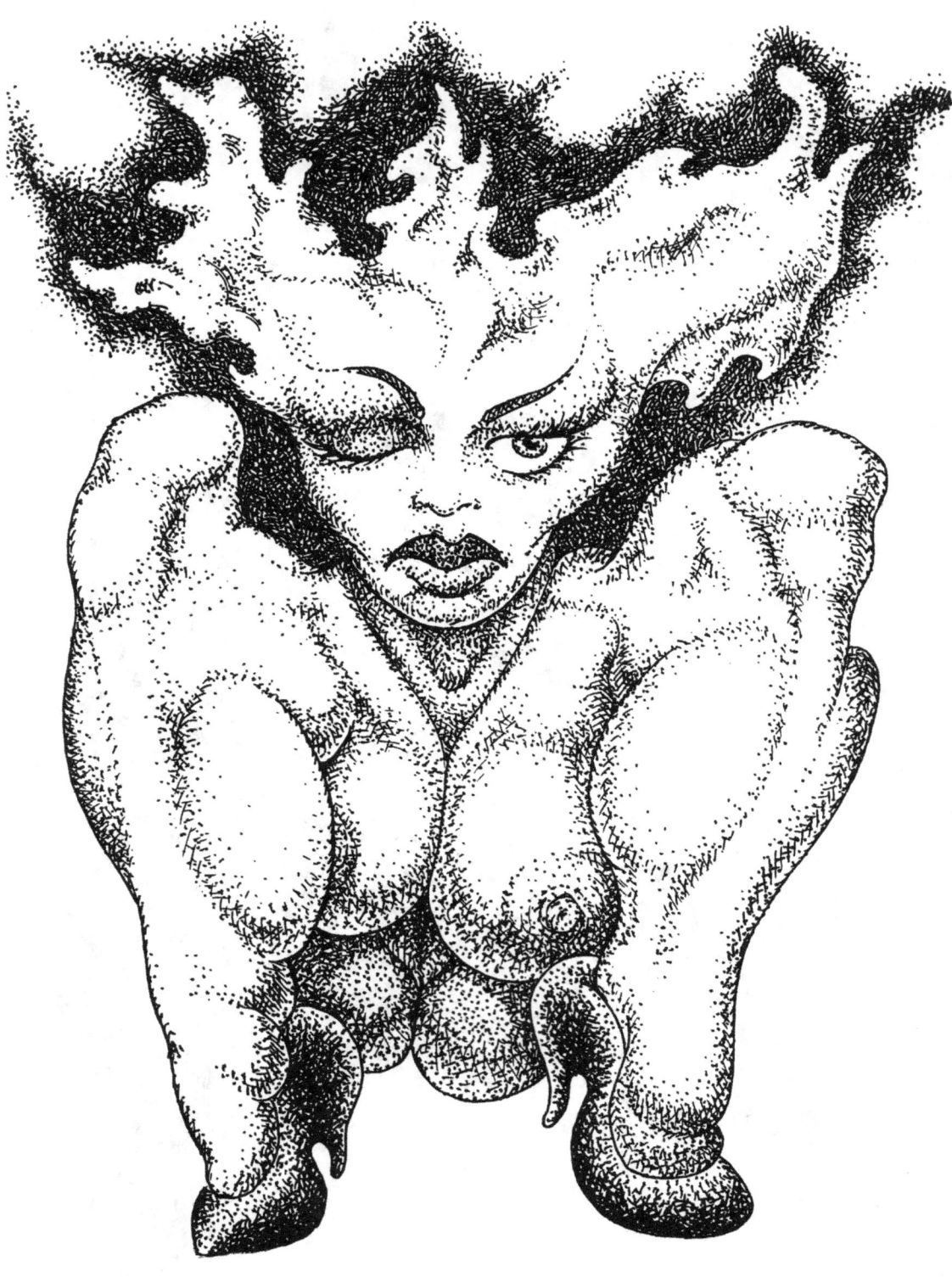

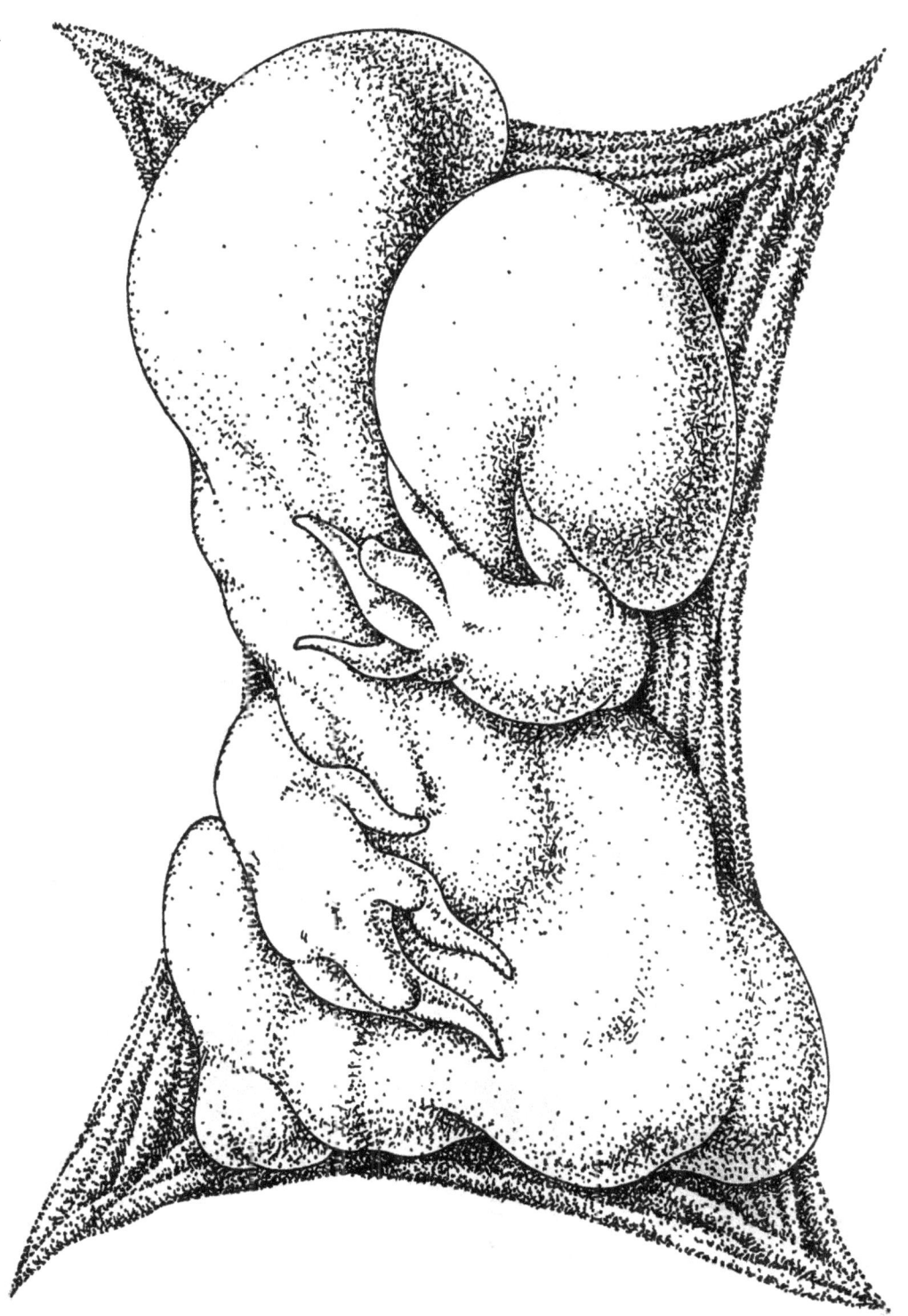

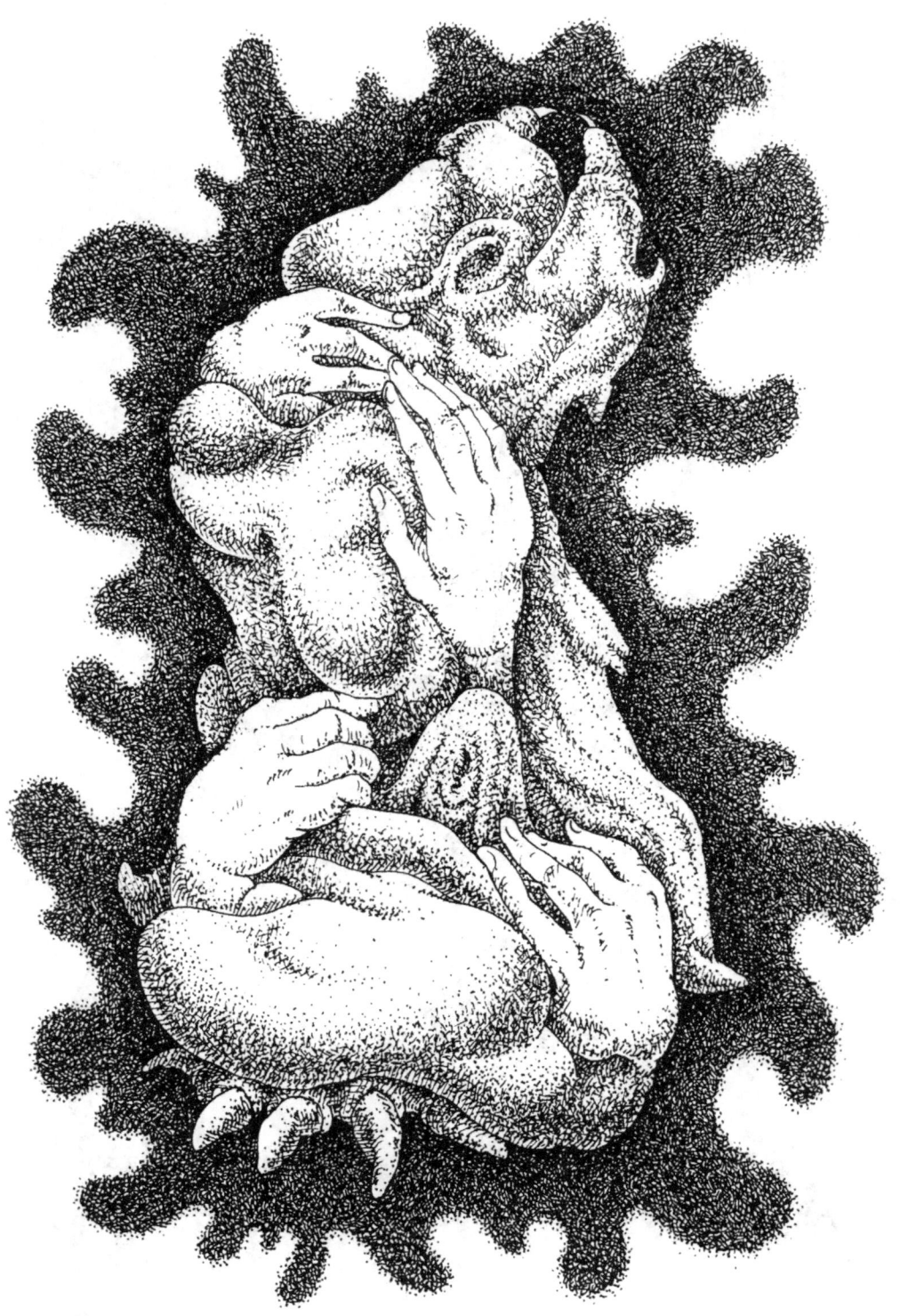

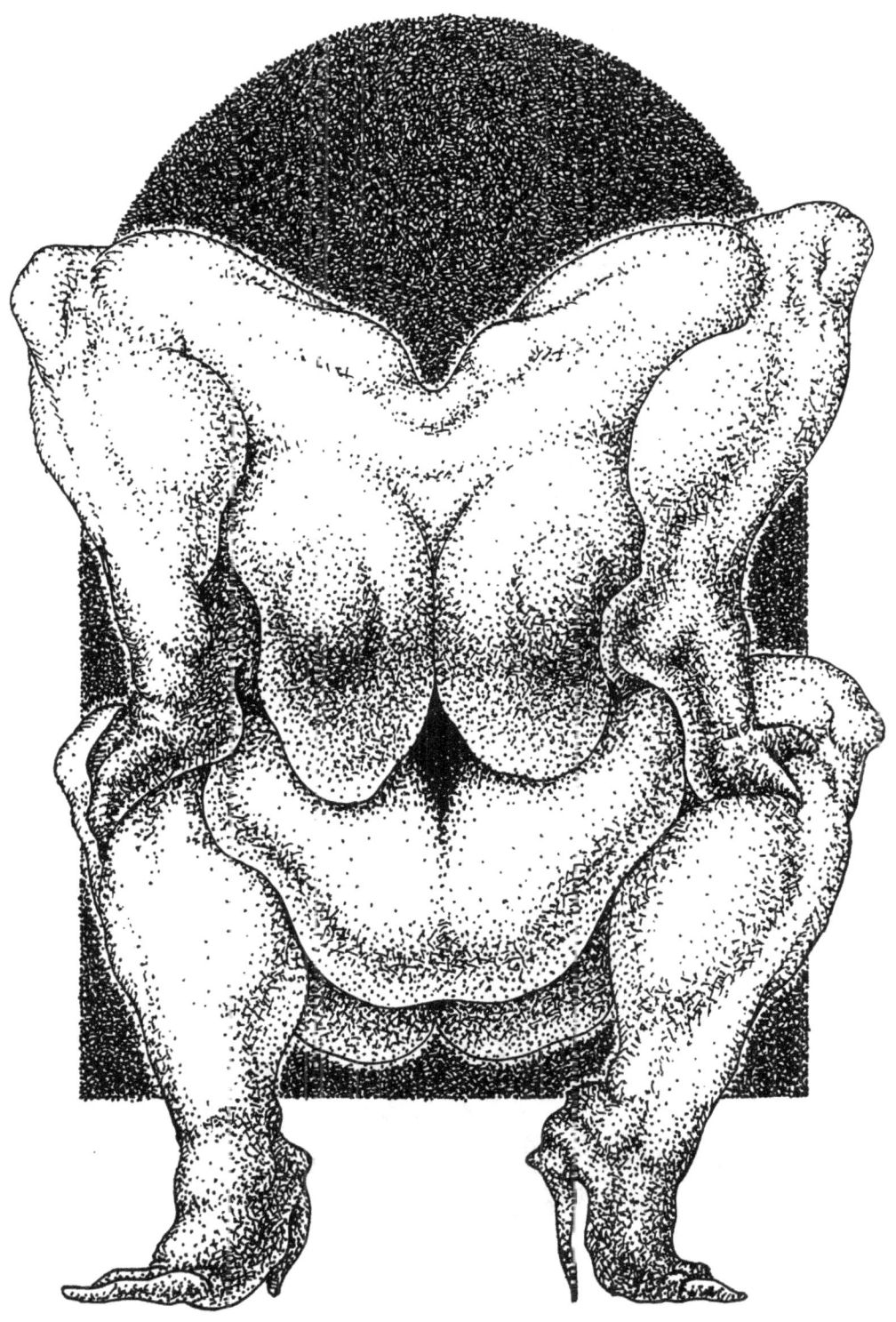

41

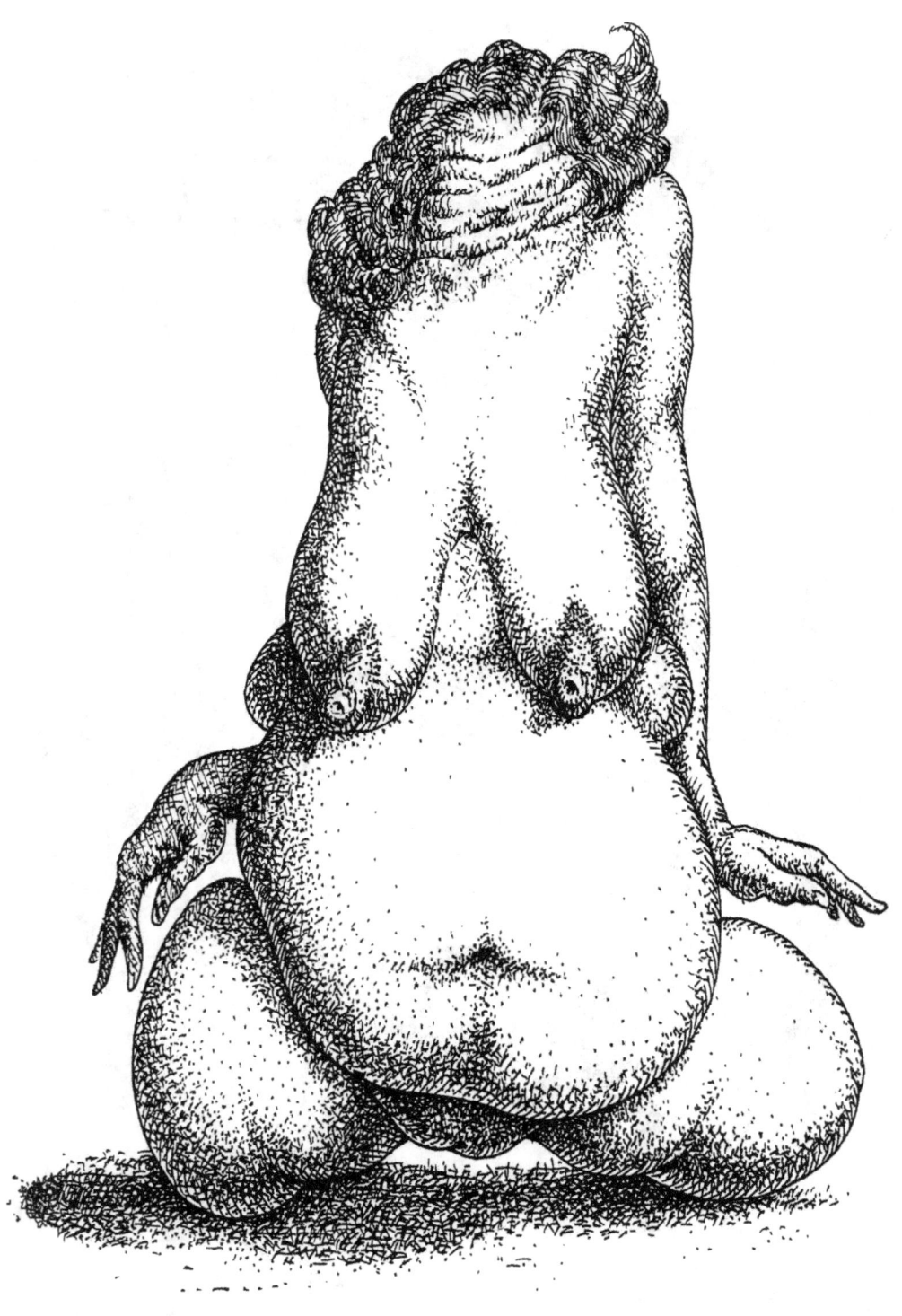

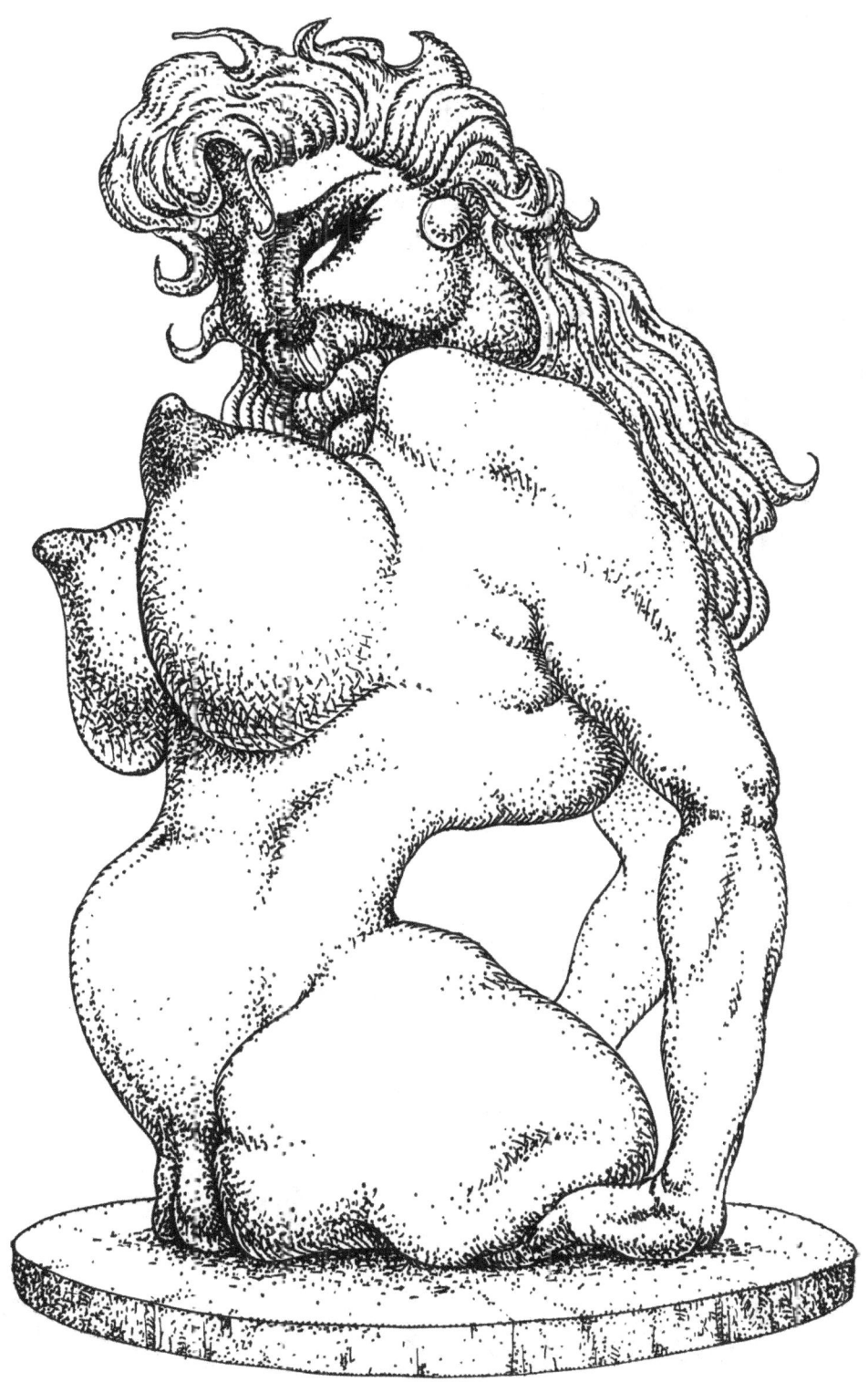

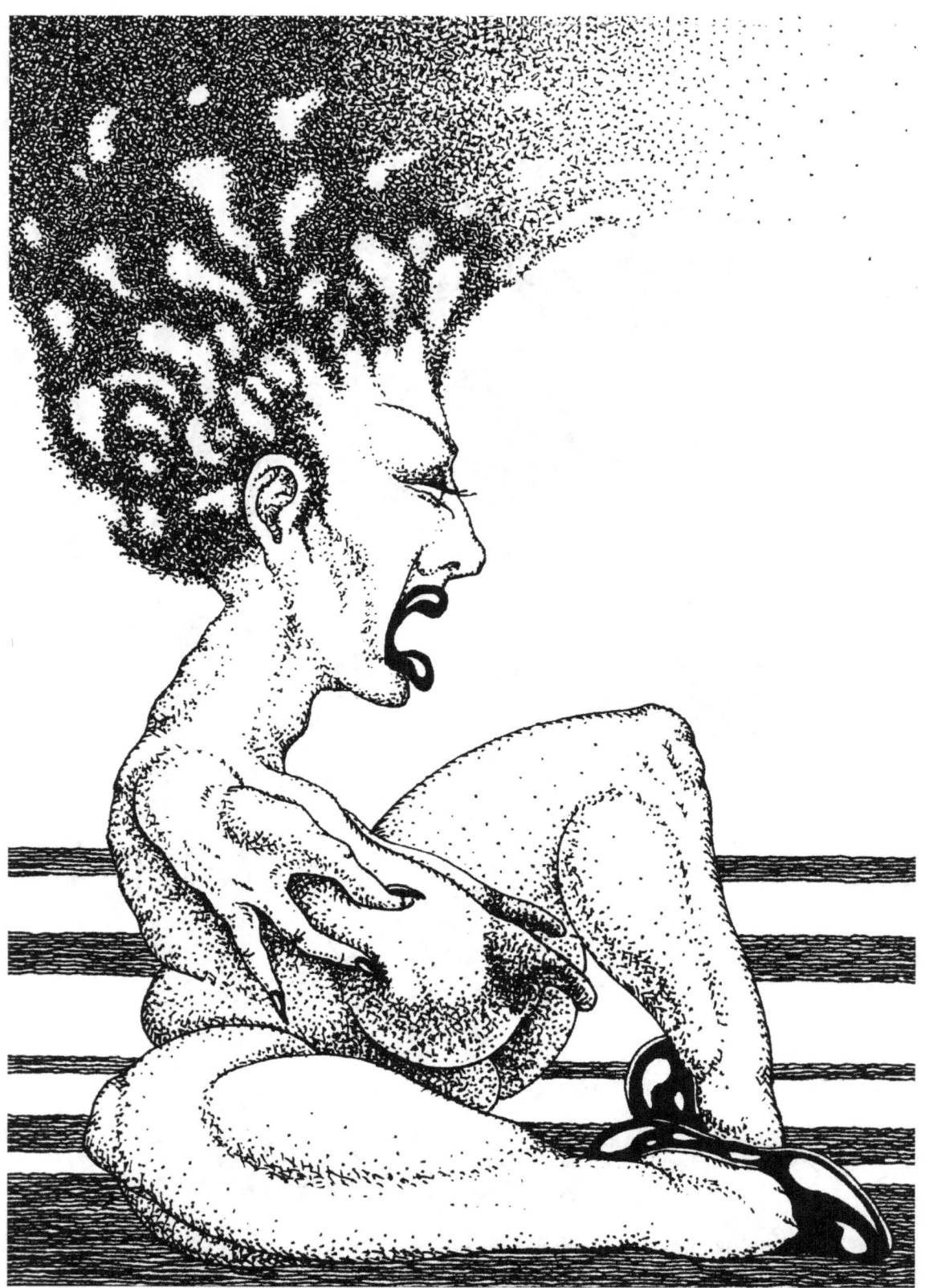

44

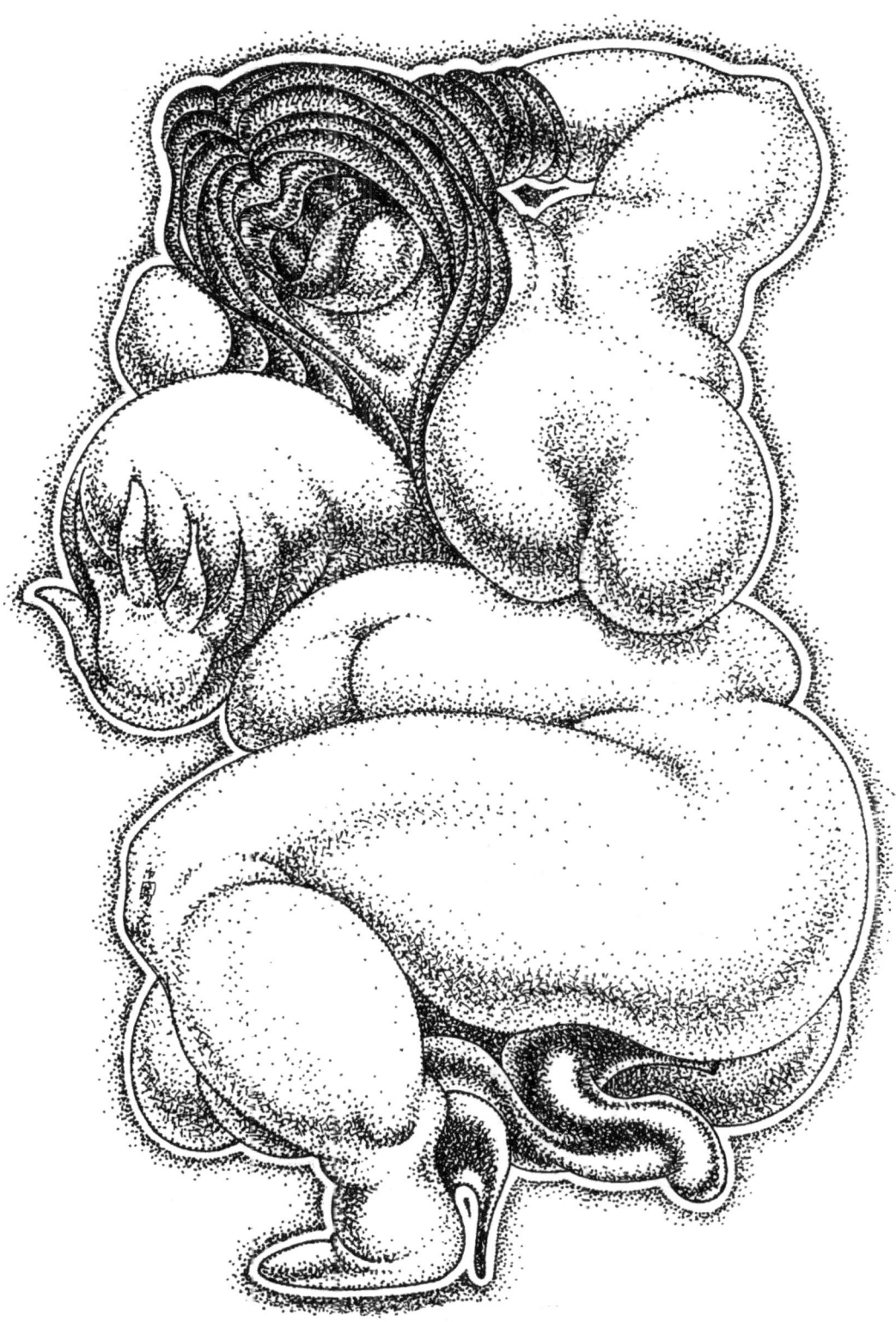

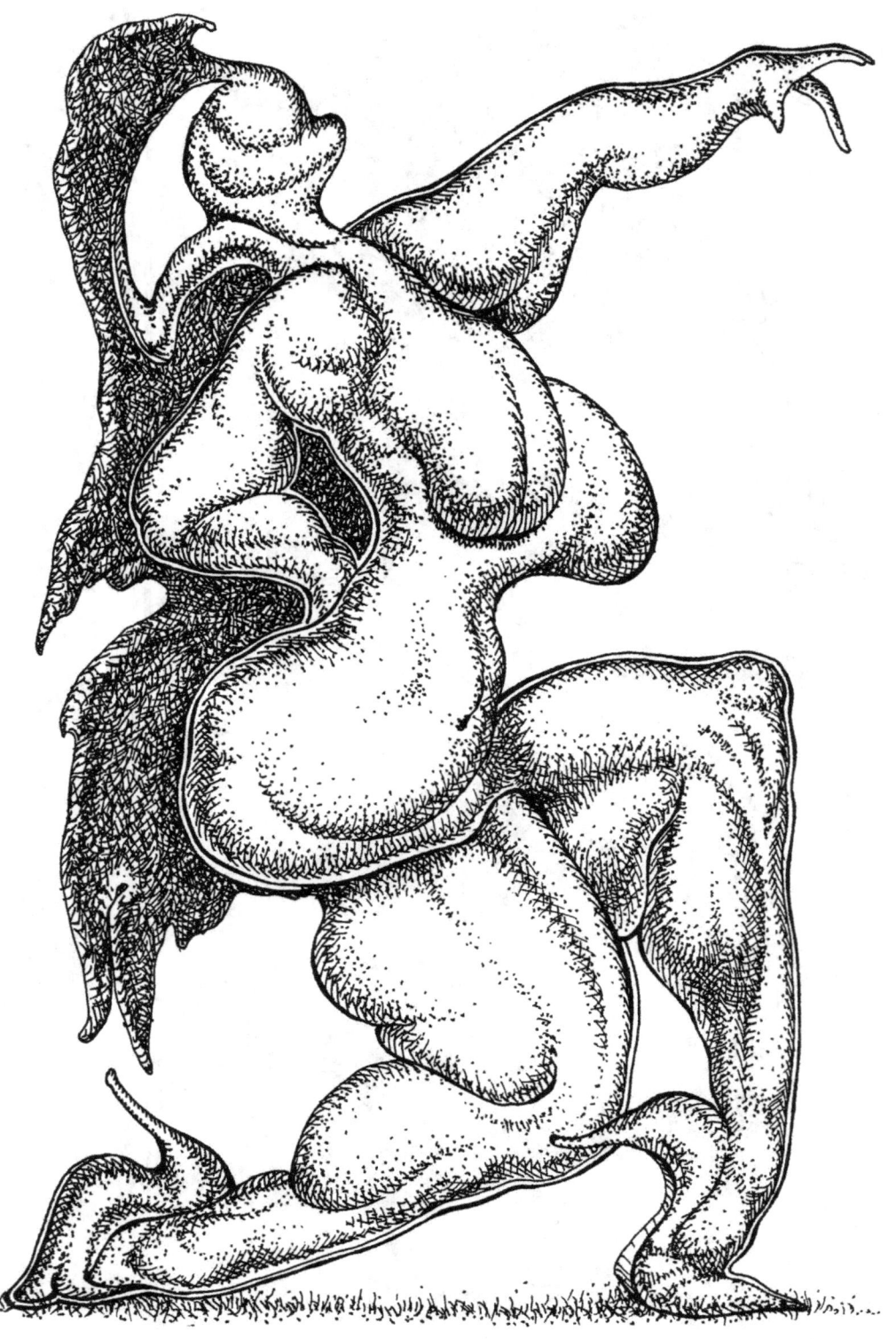

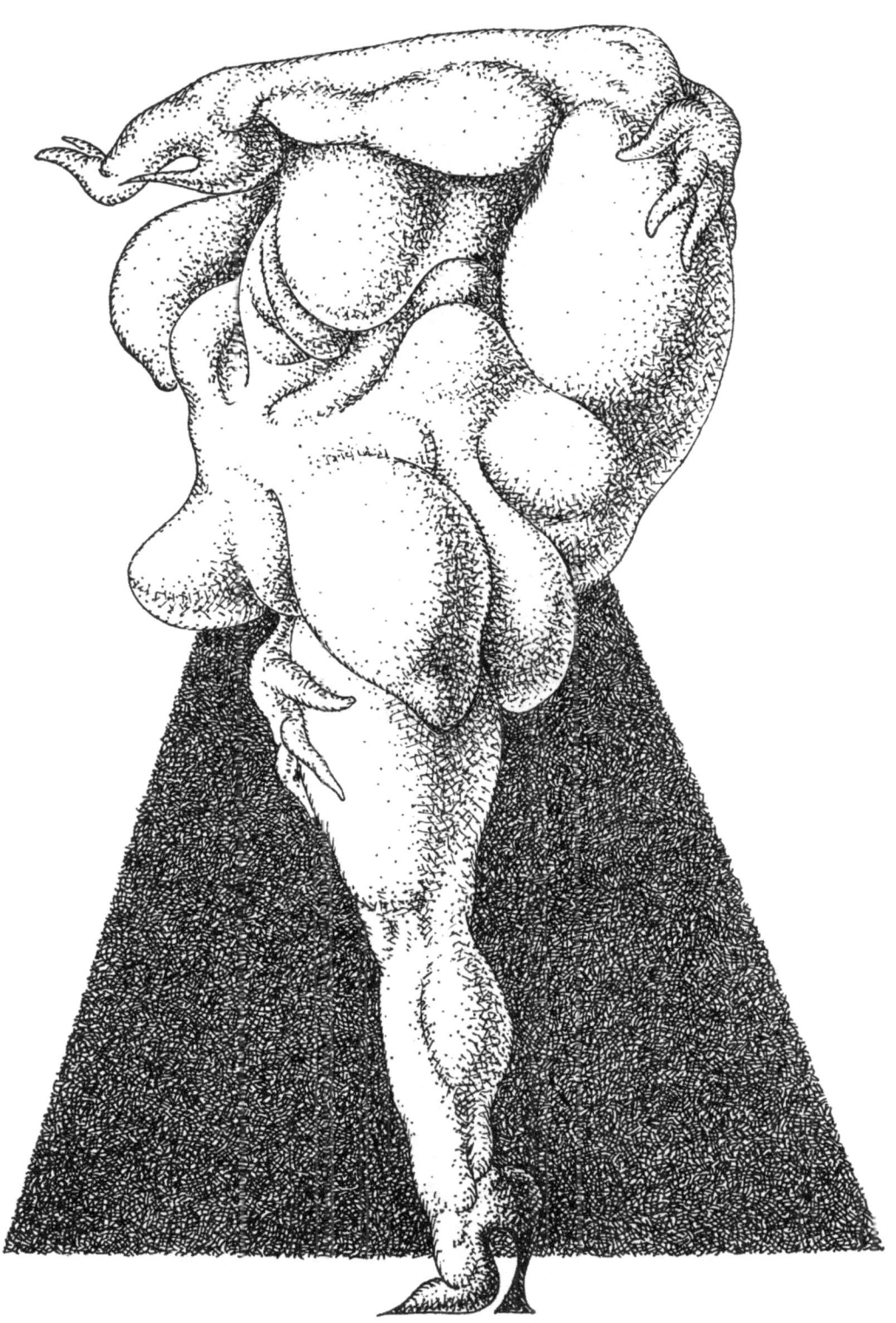

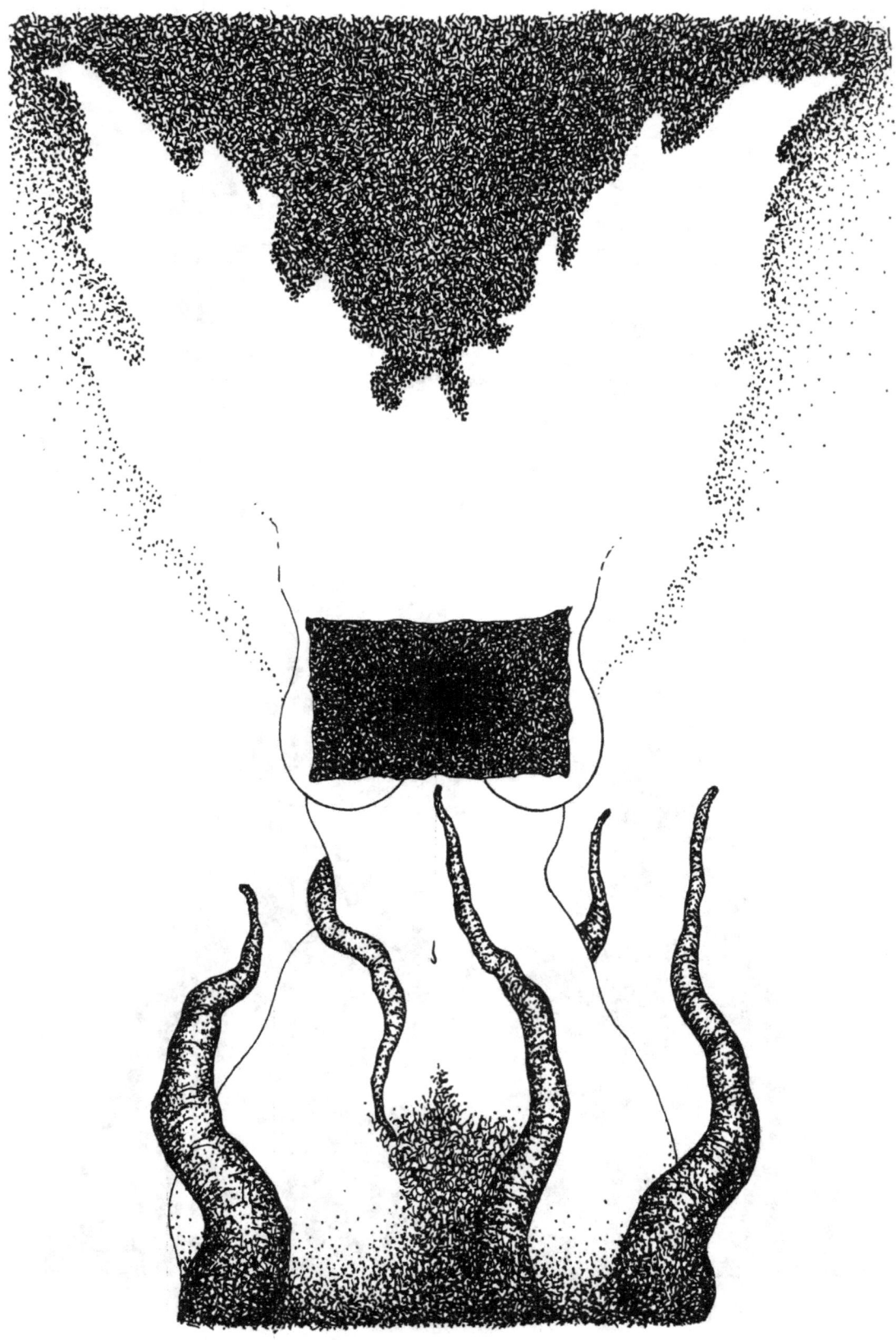

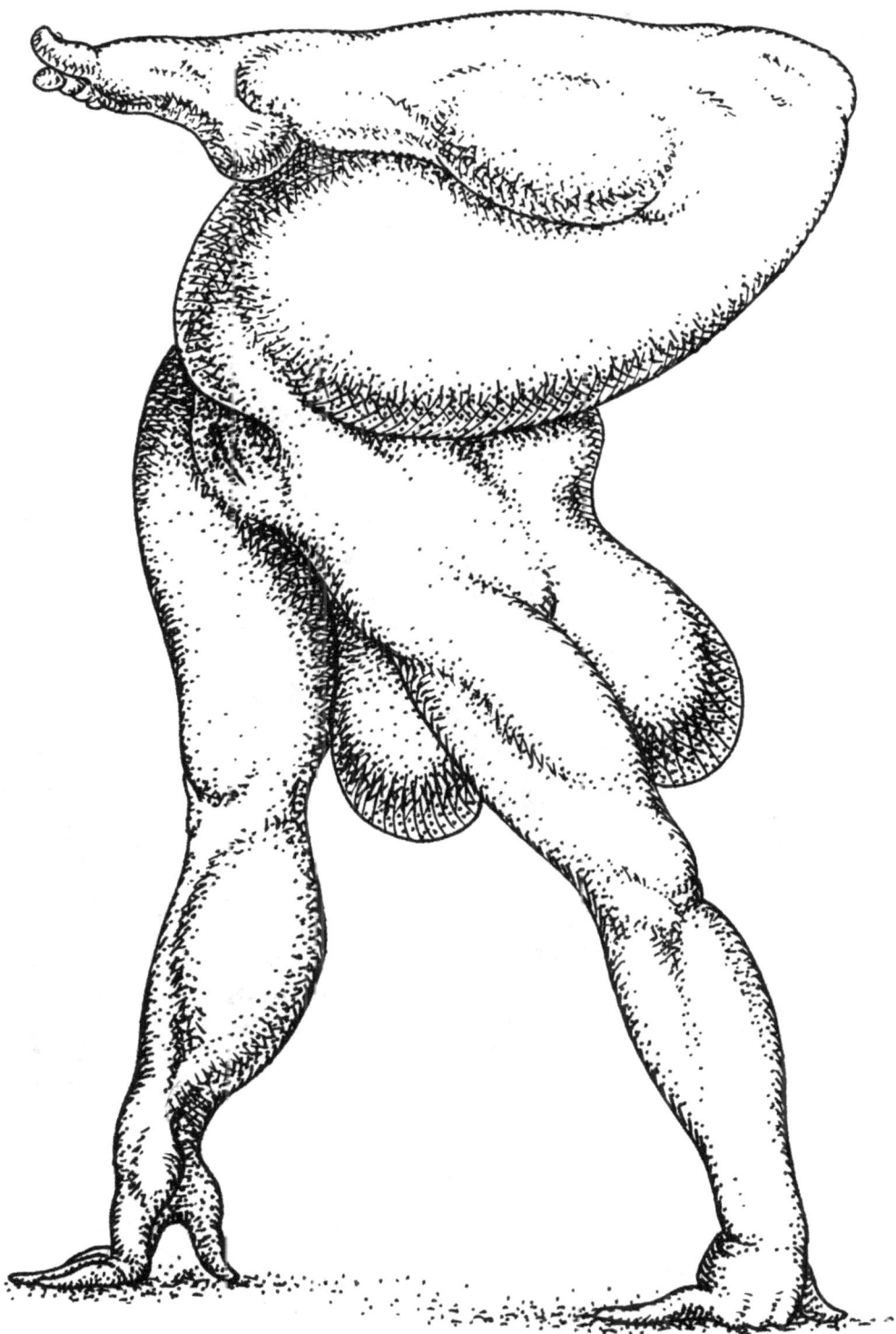

49

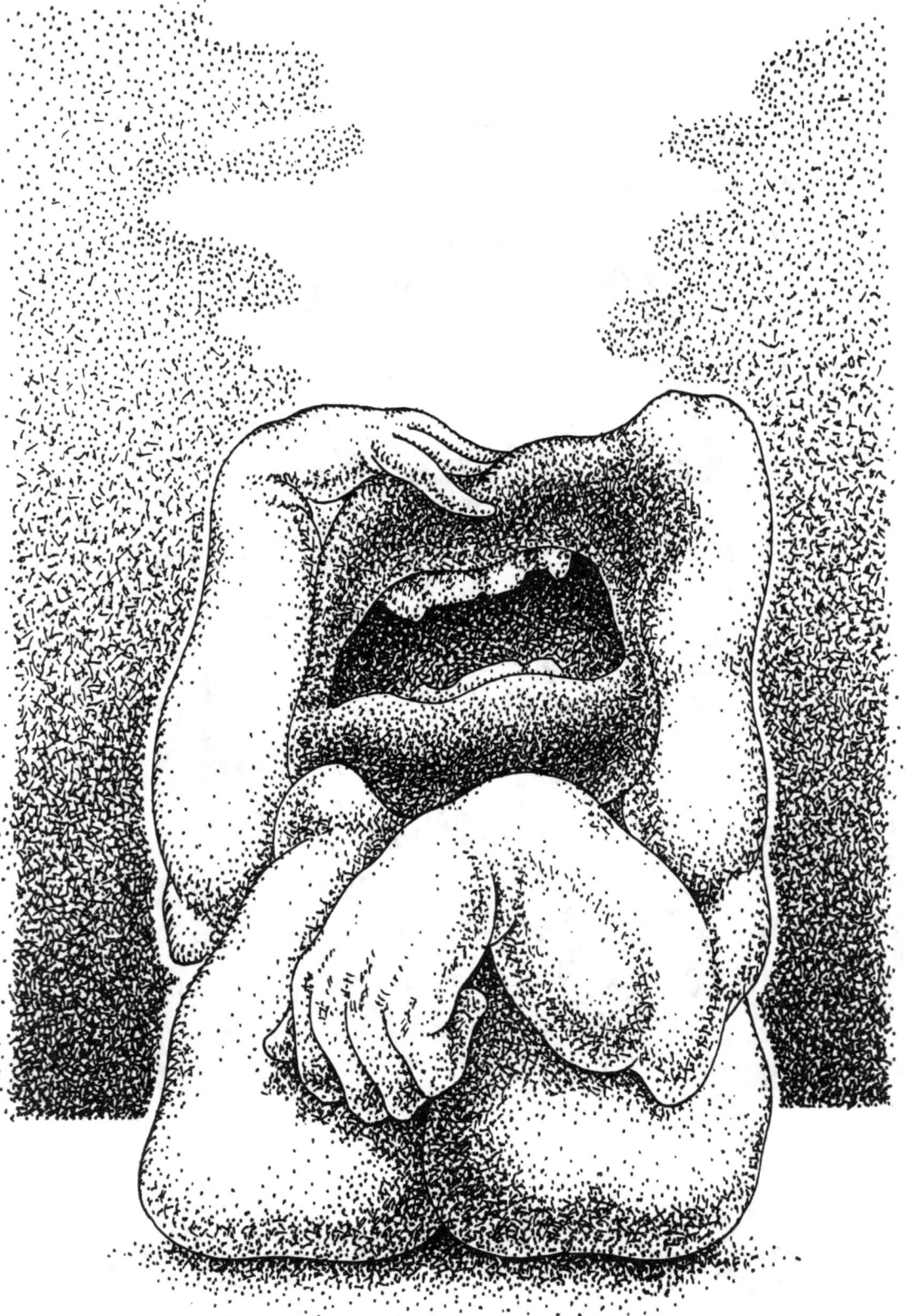

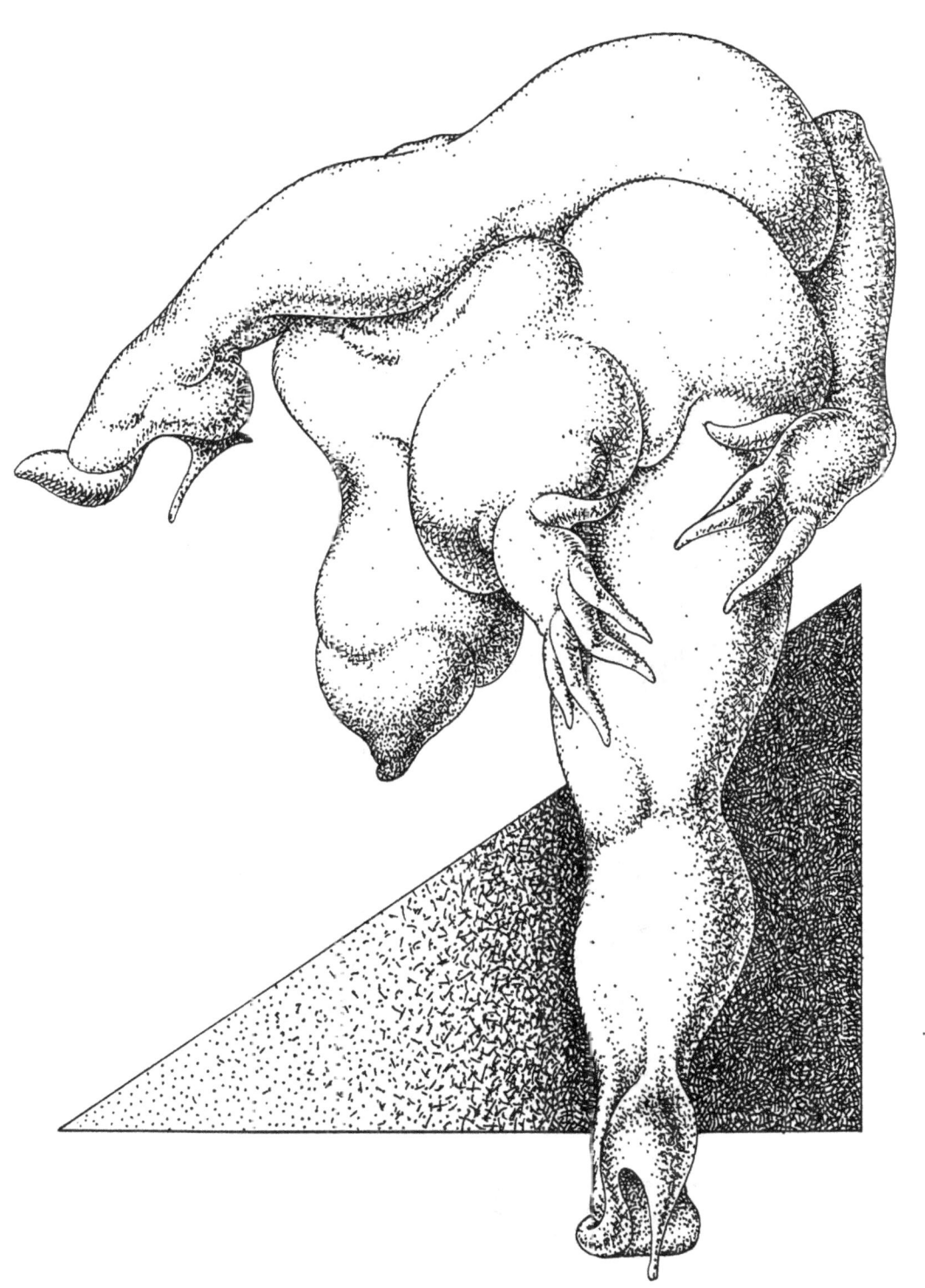

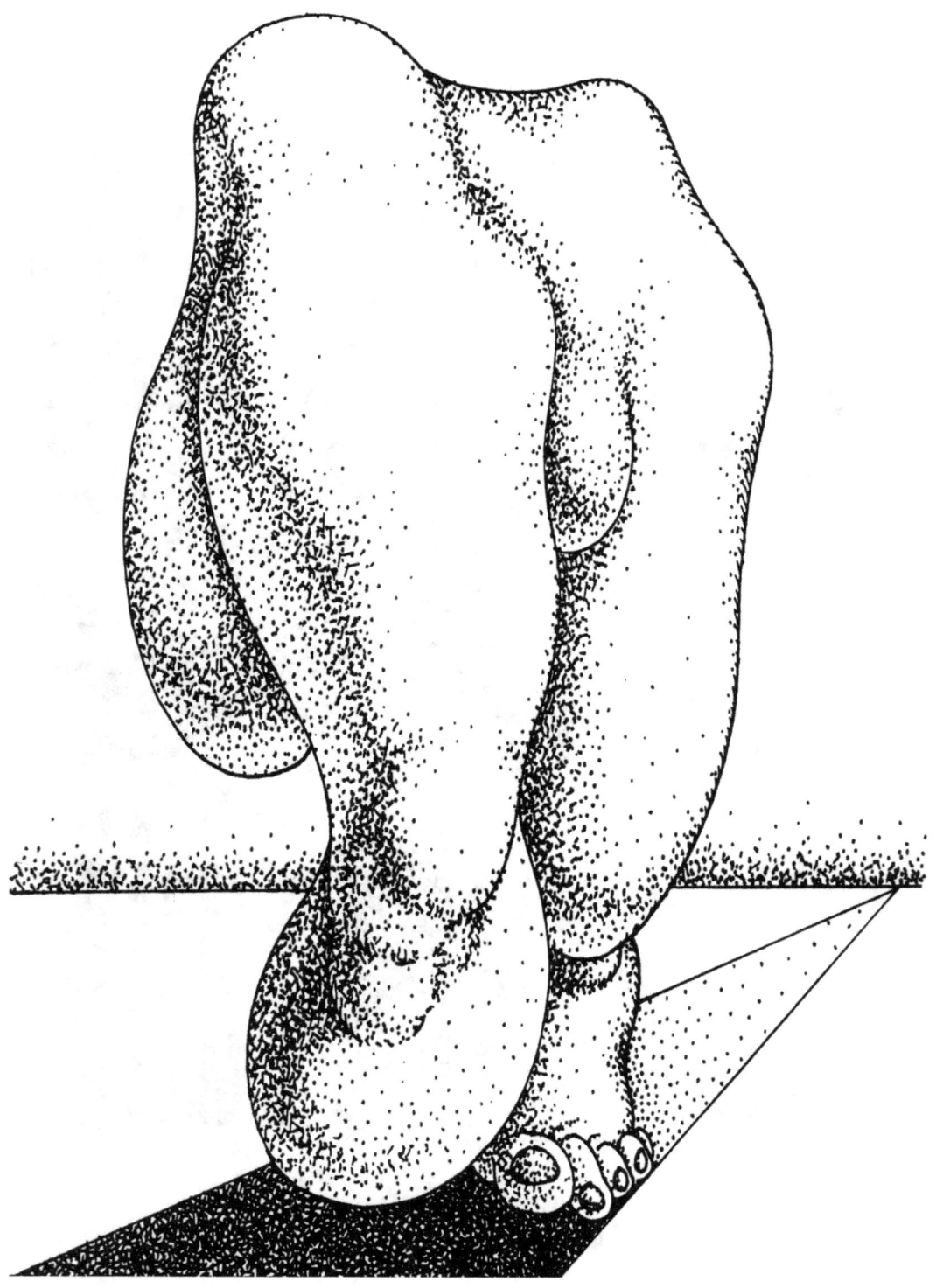

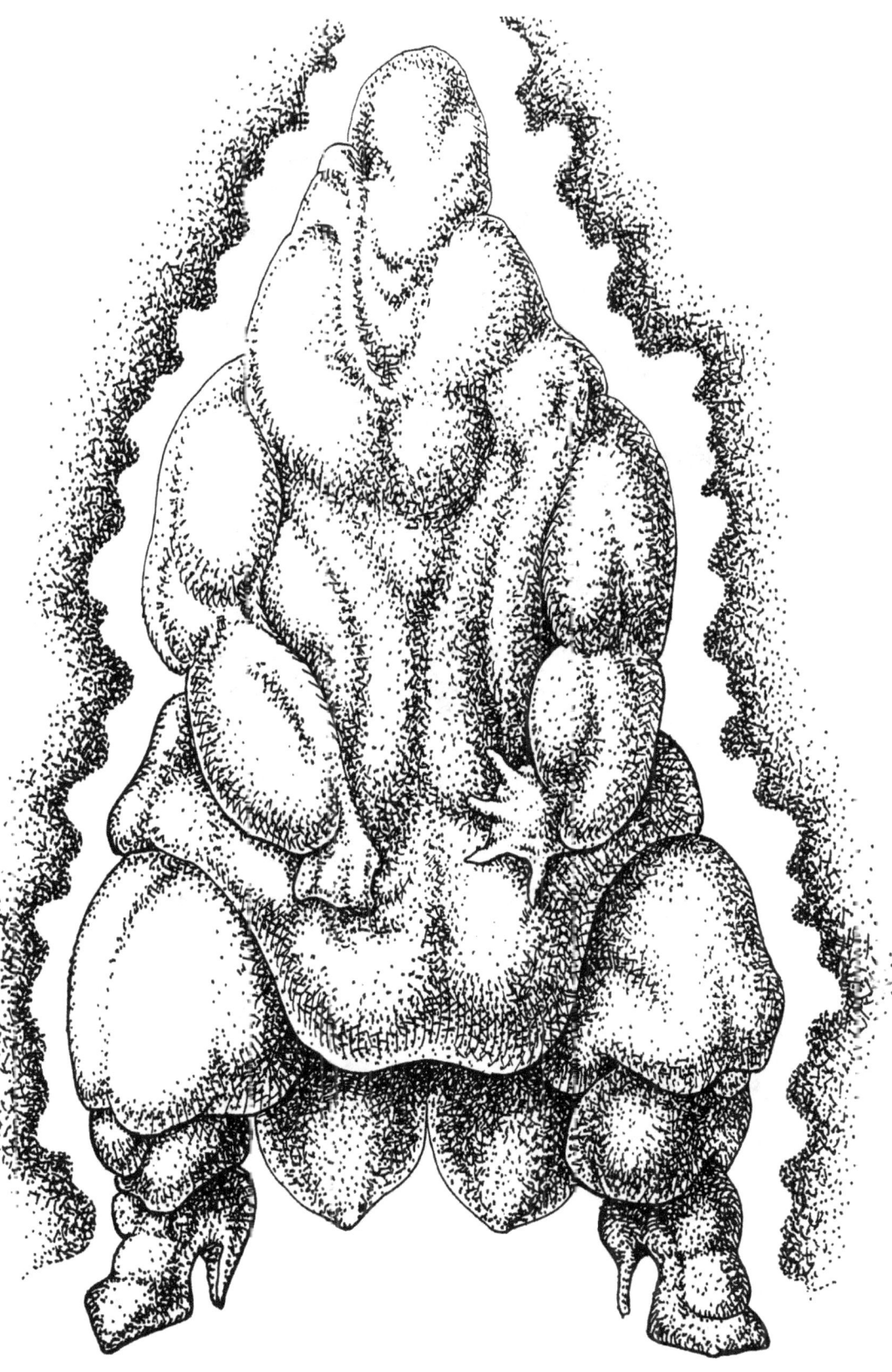

53

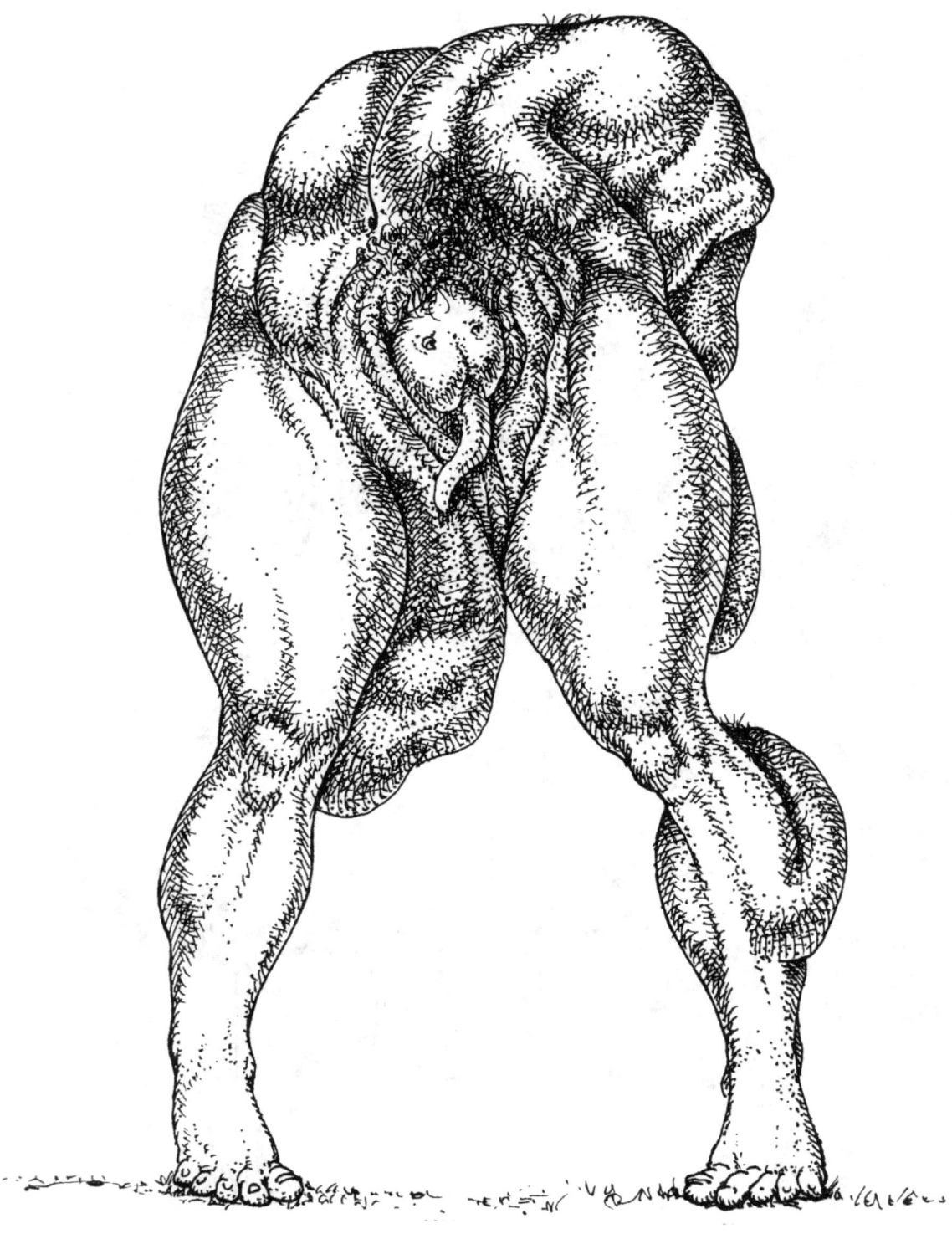

54

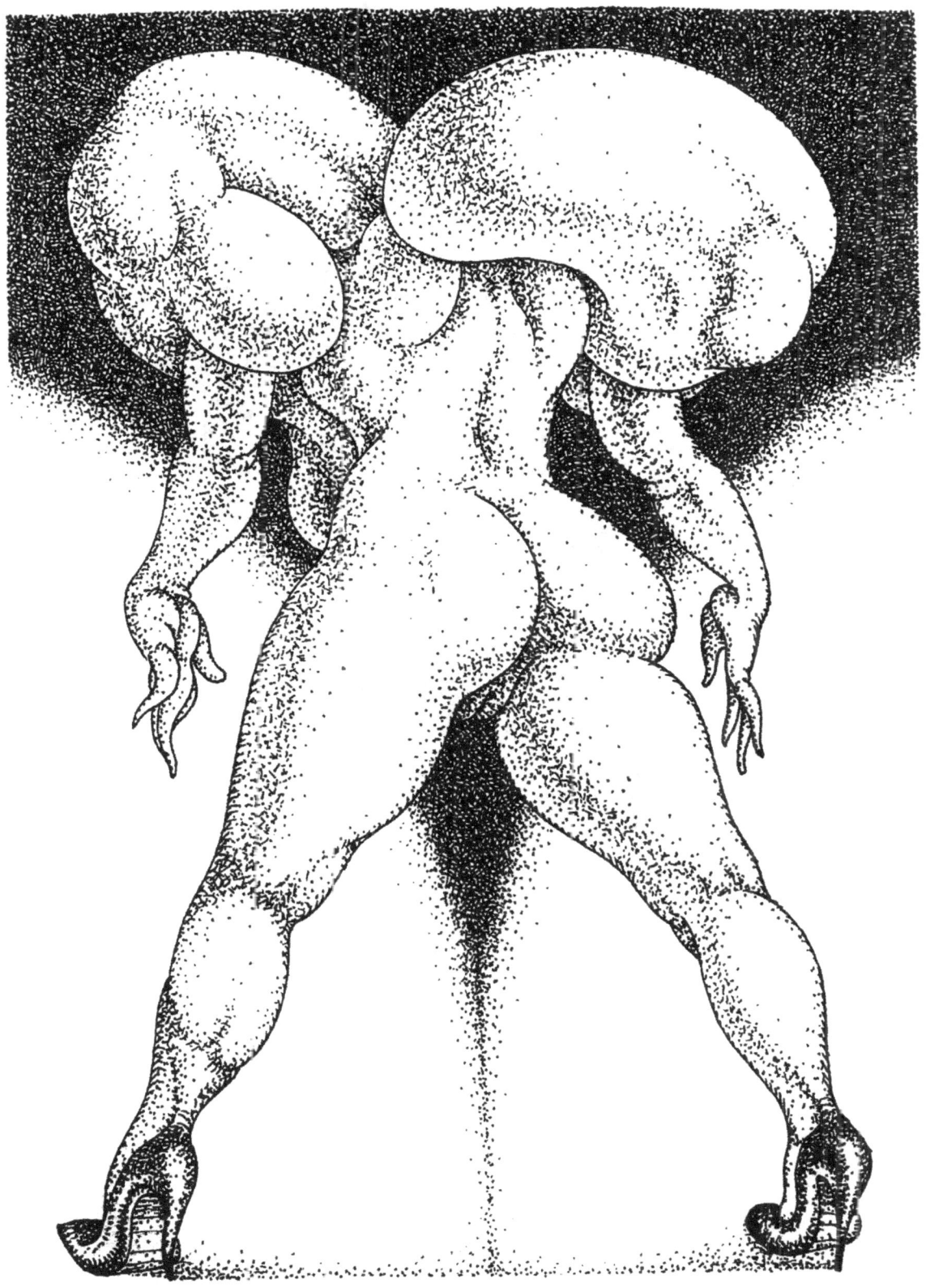

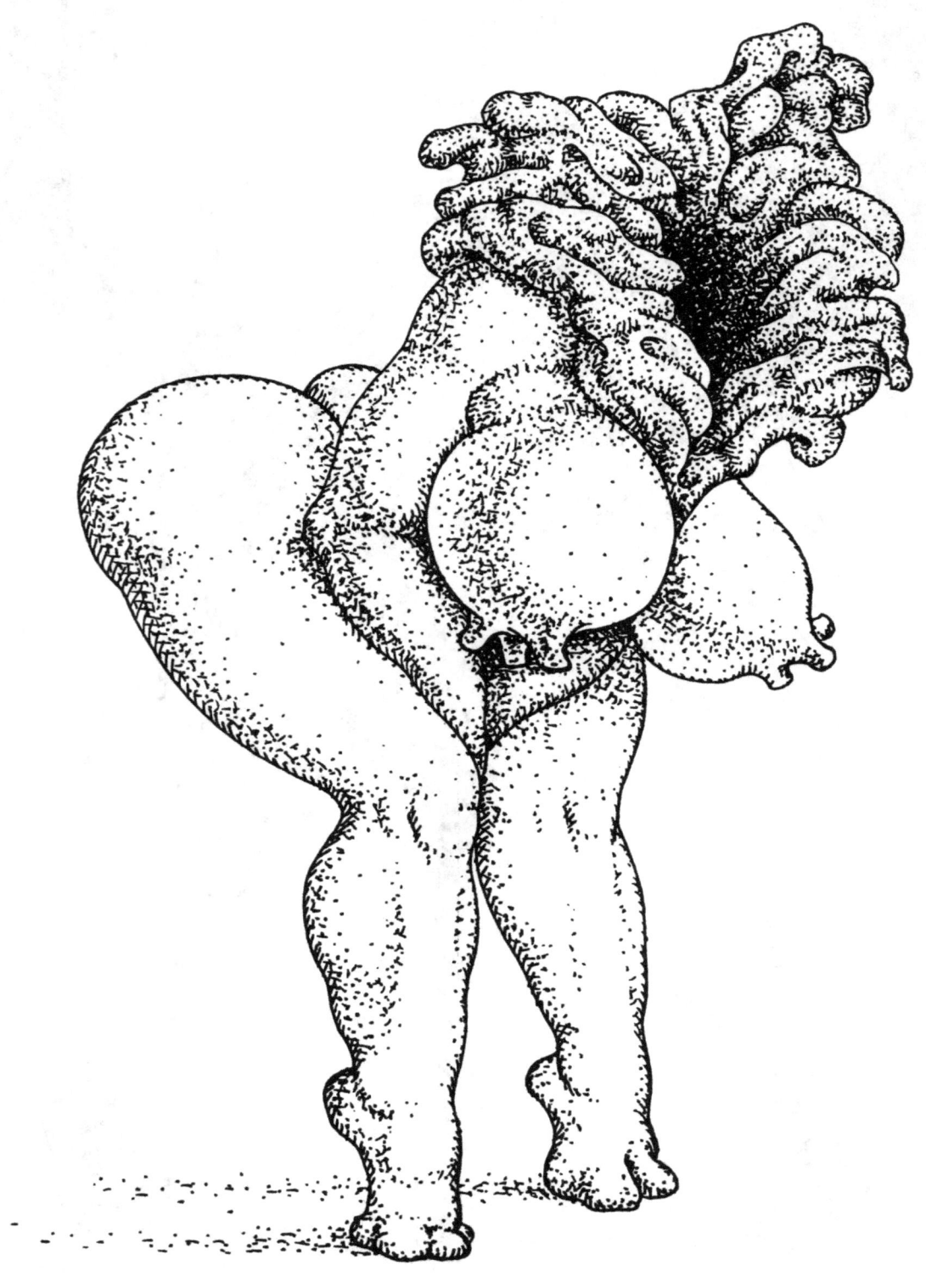

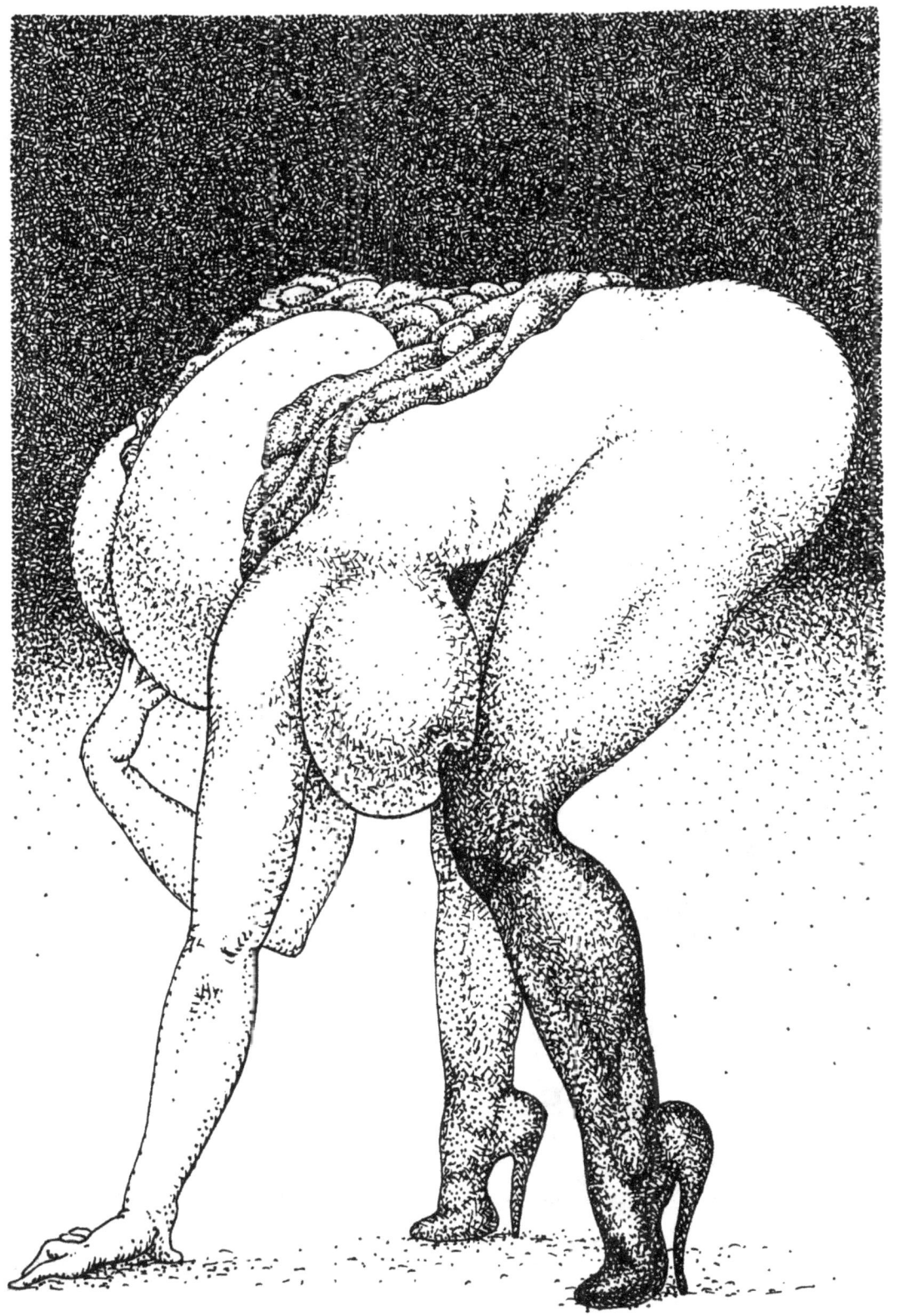

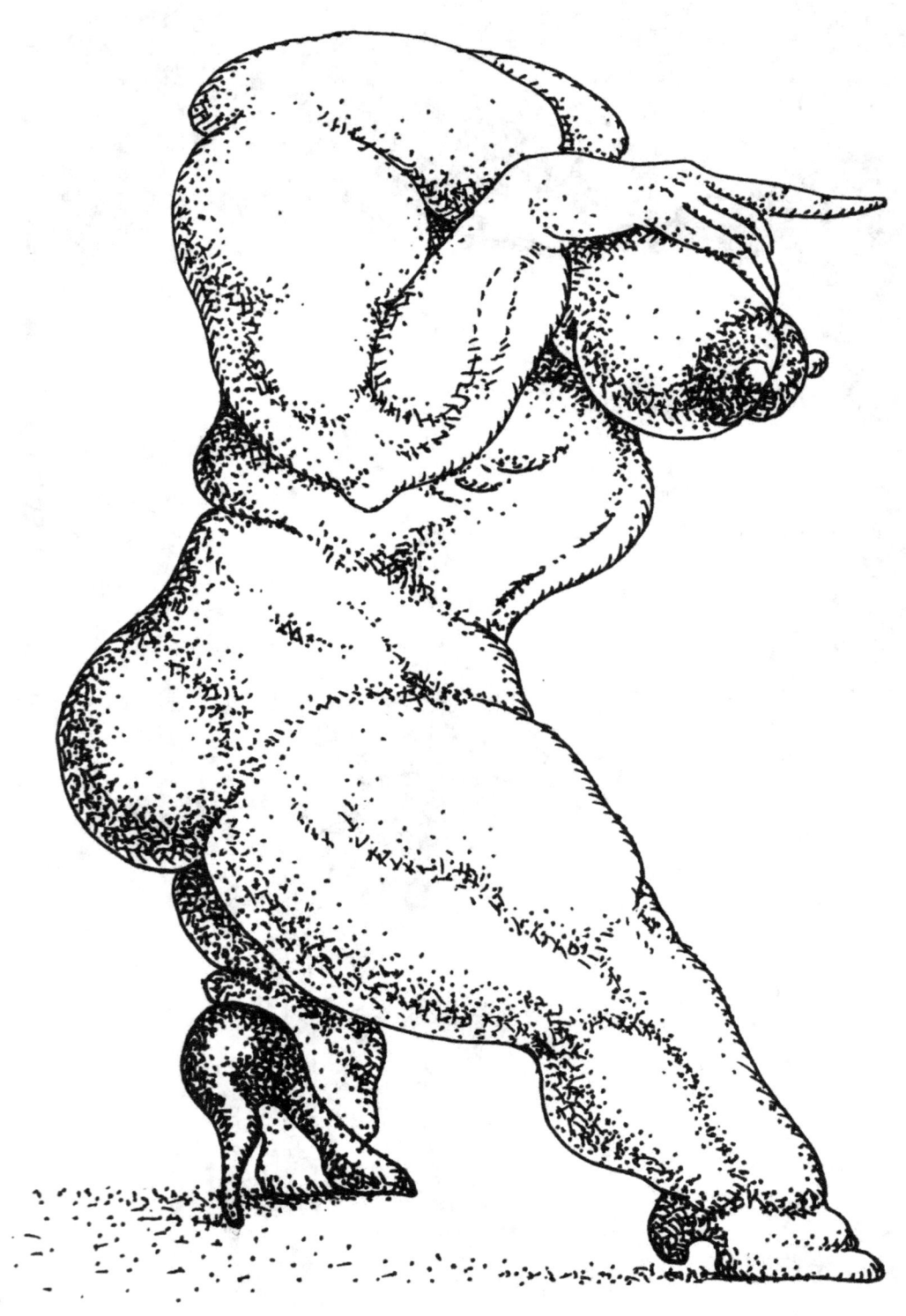

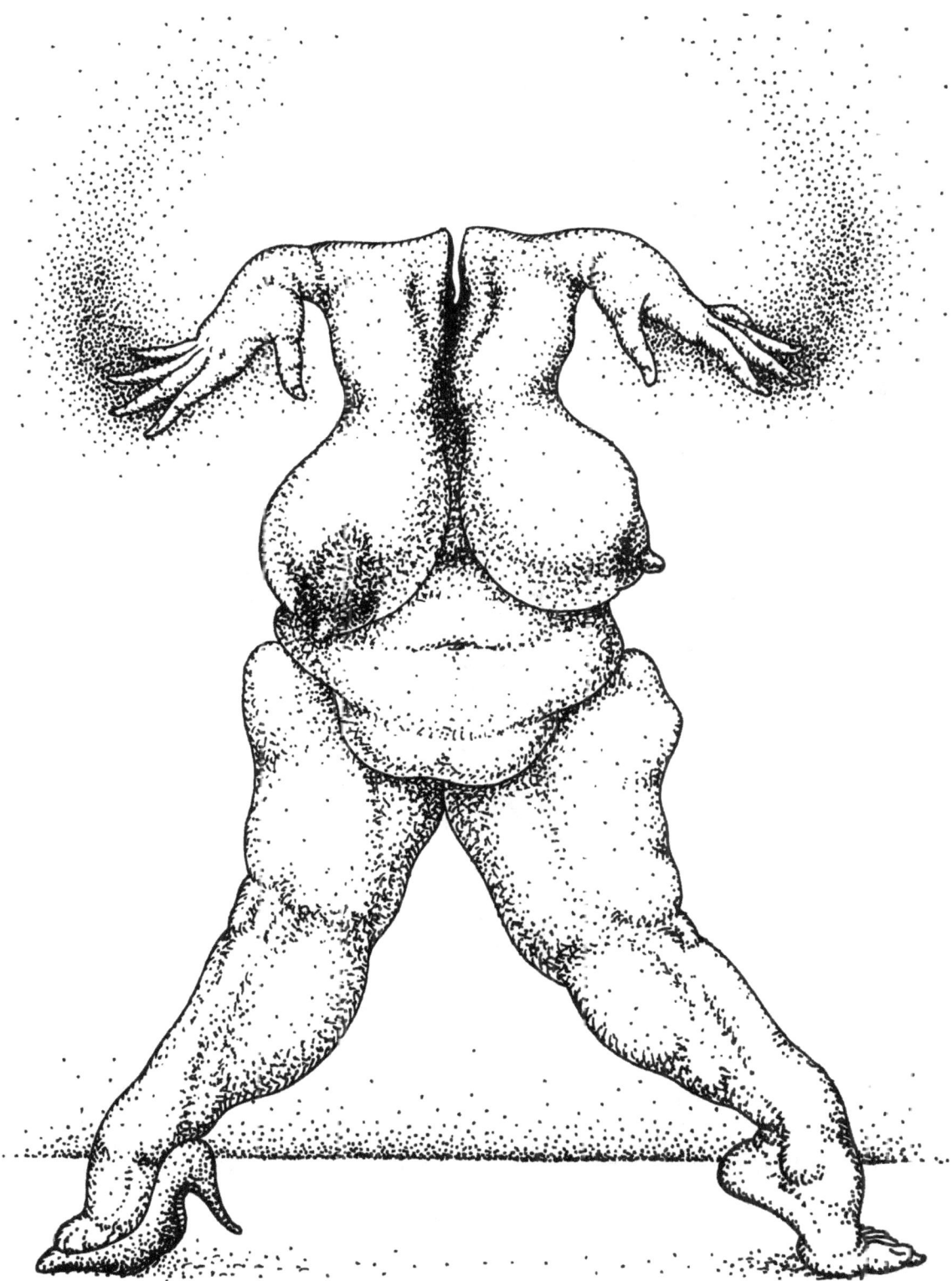

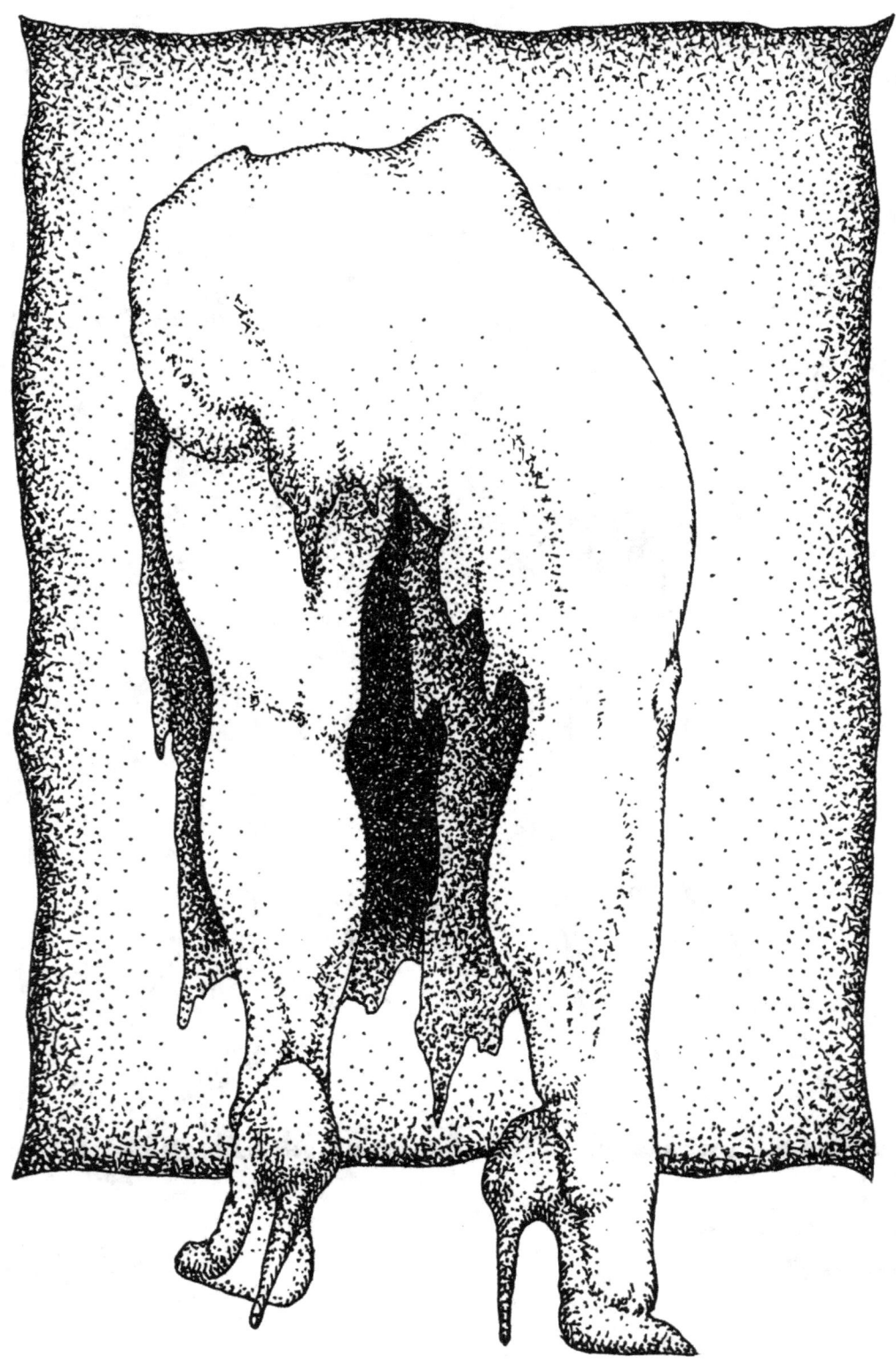

60

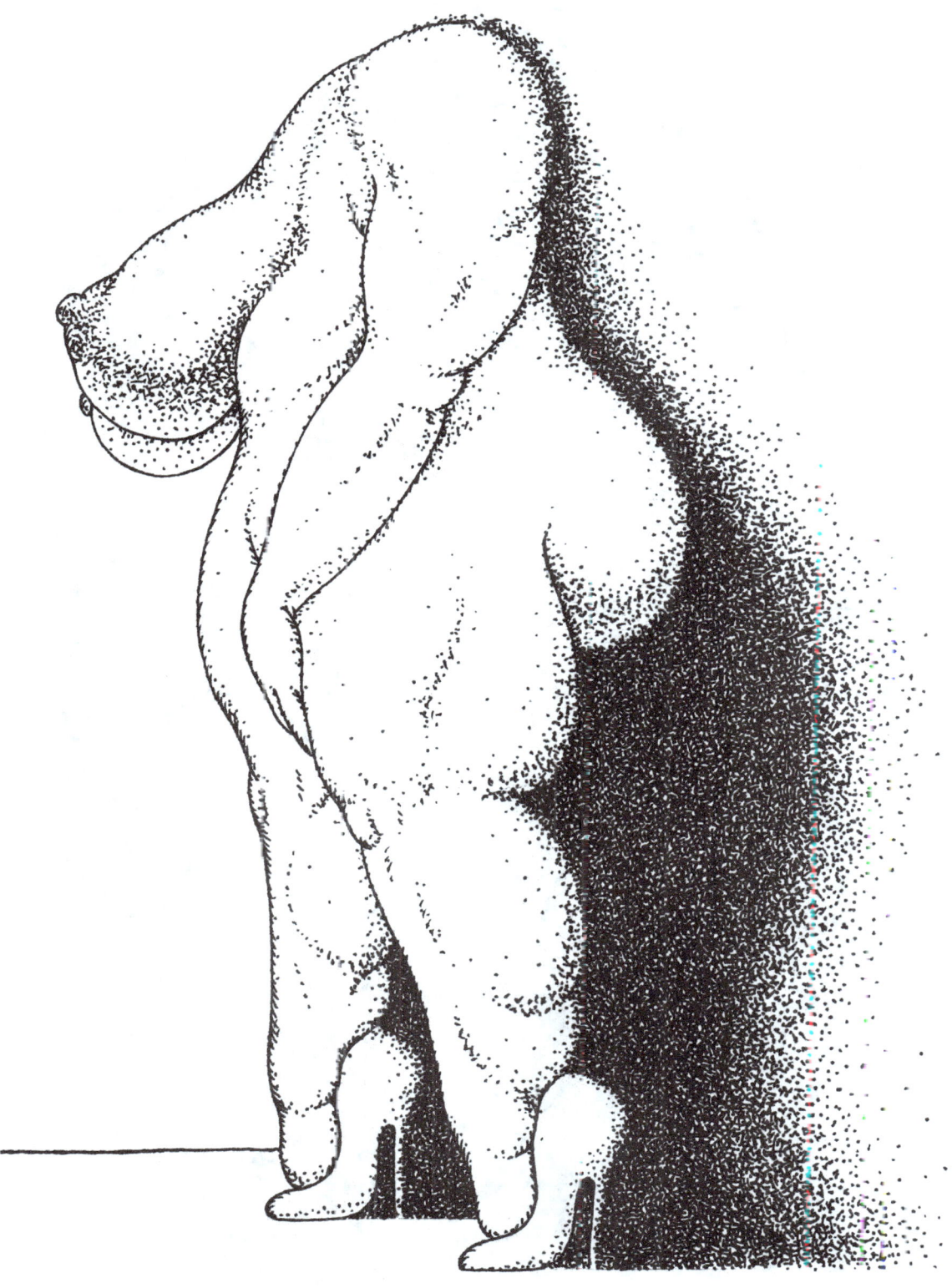

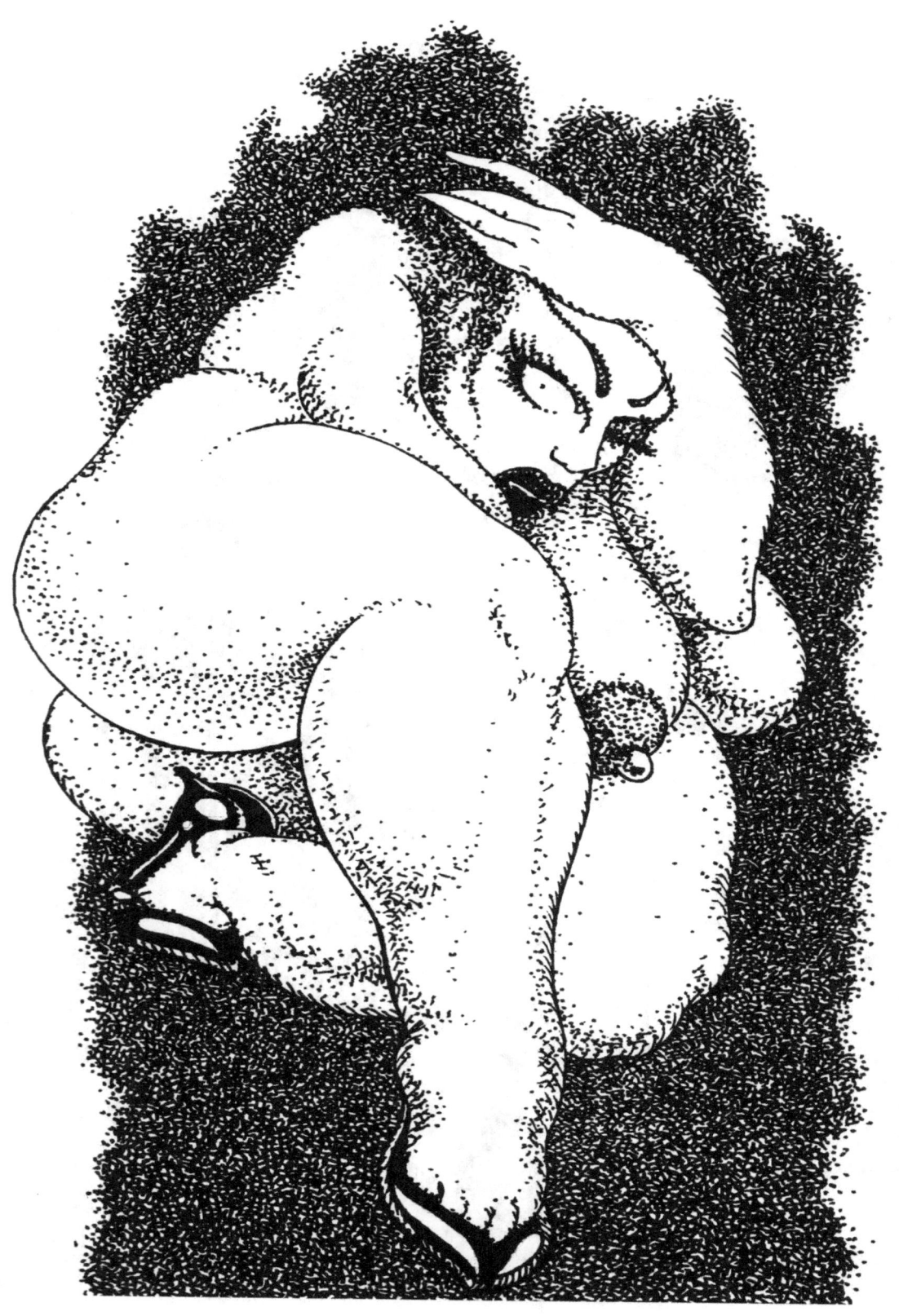

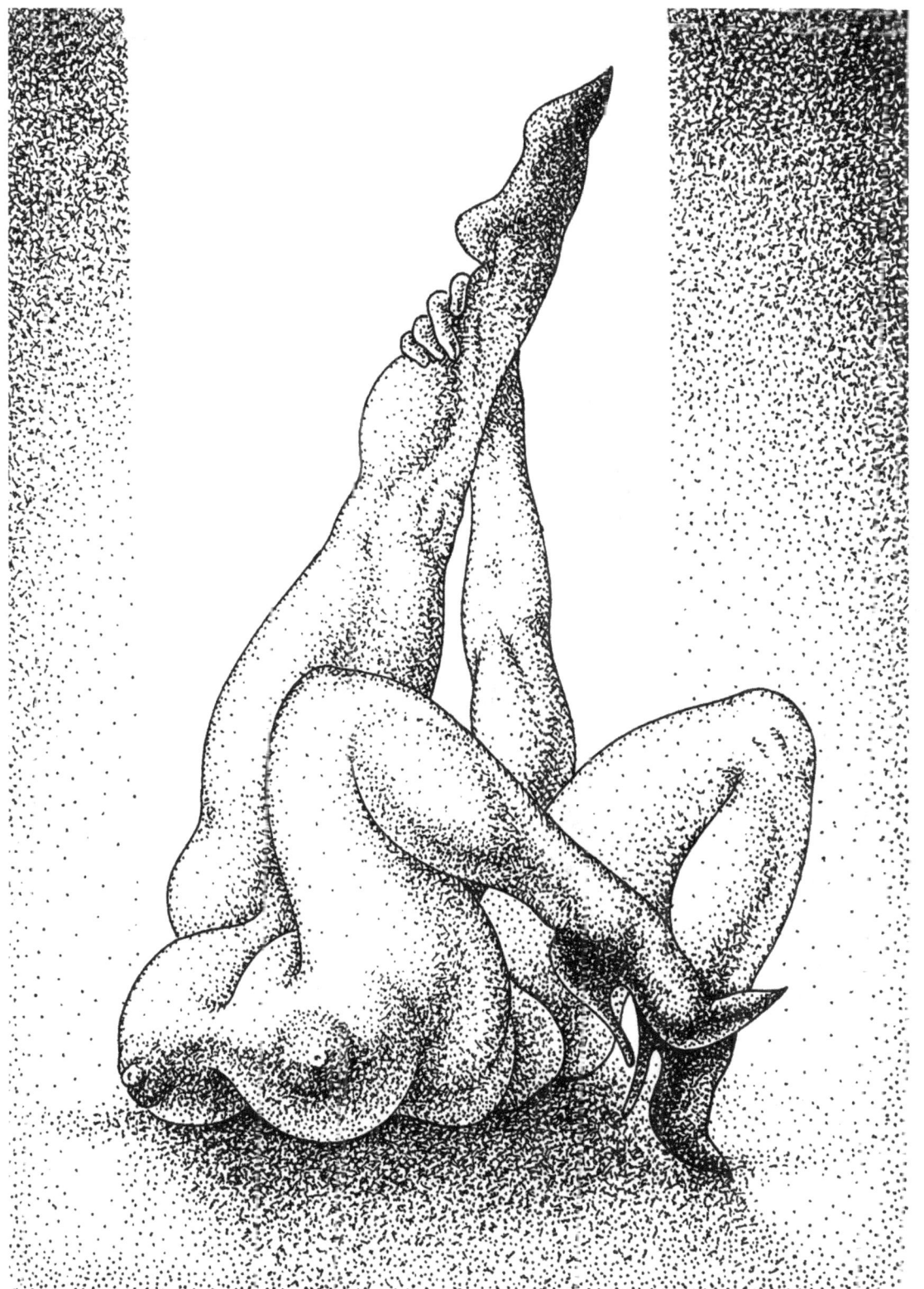

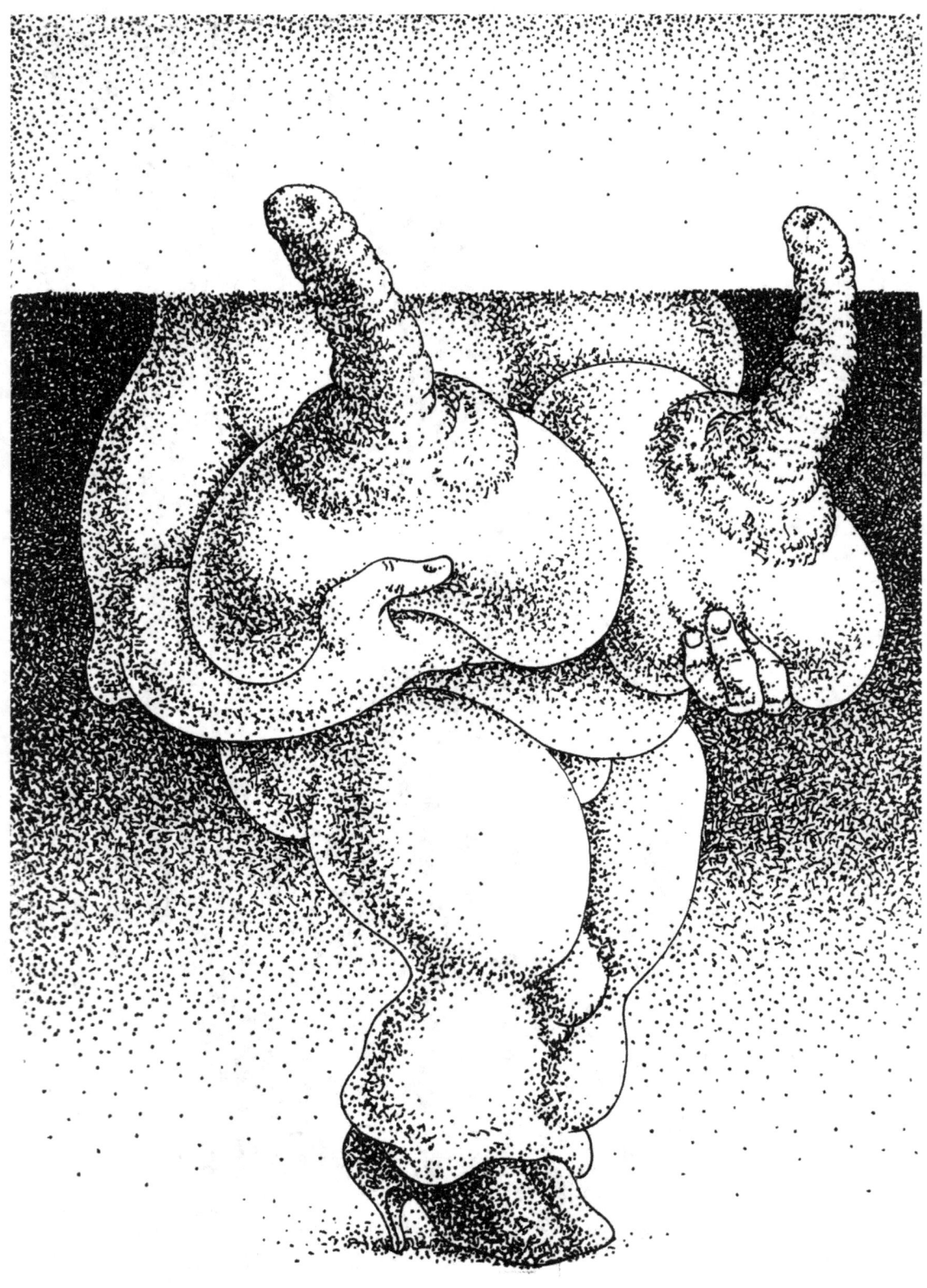

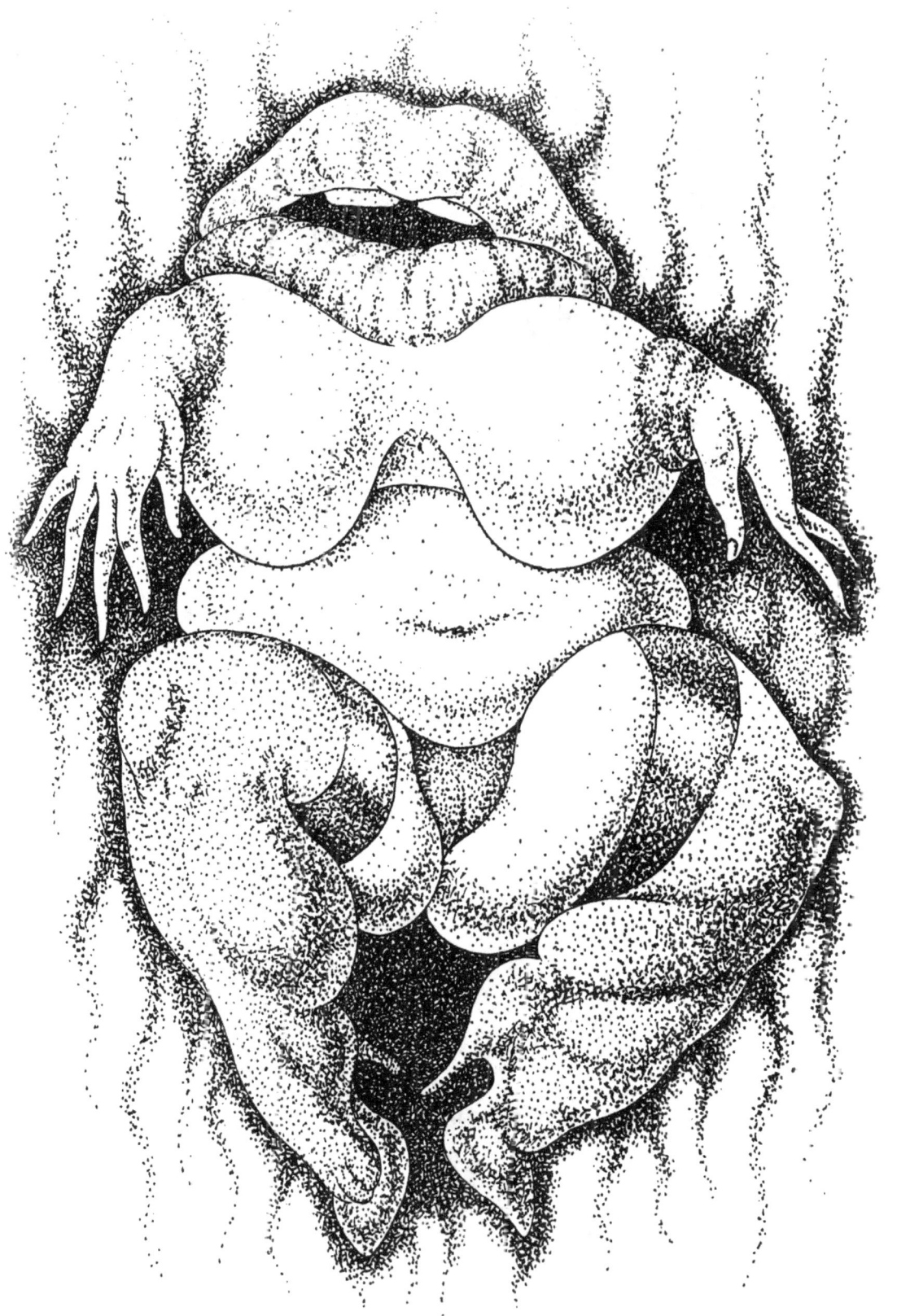

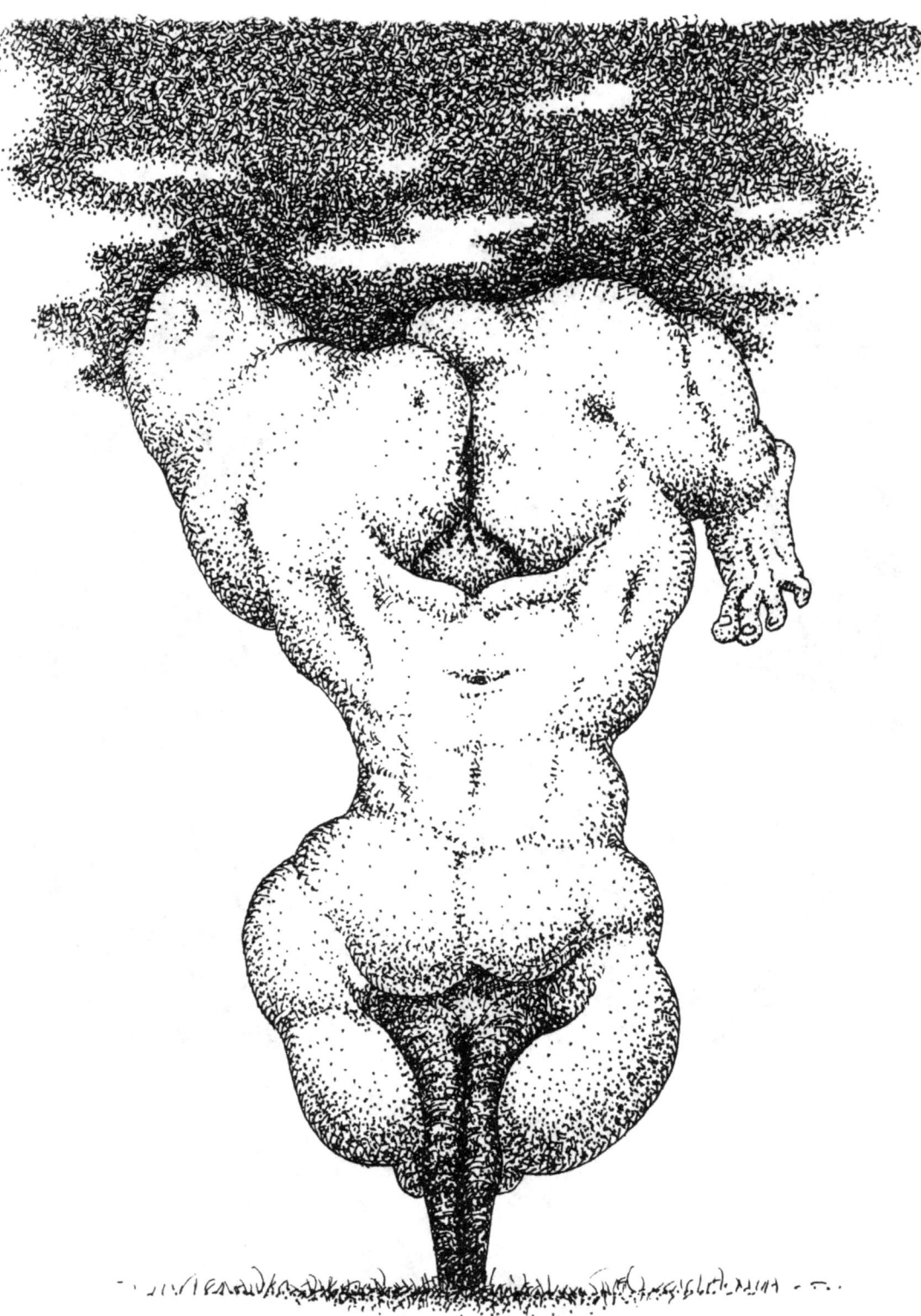

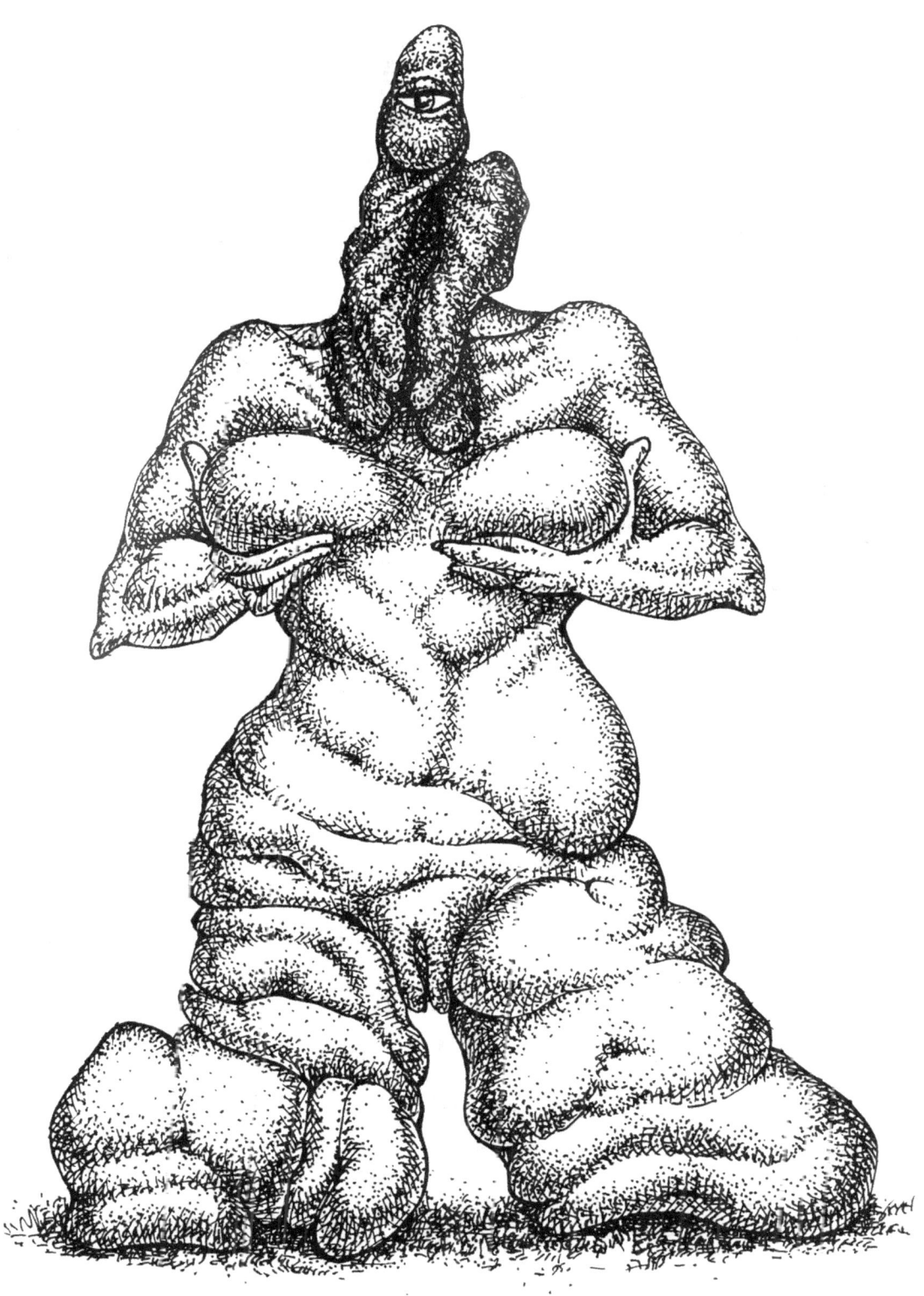

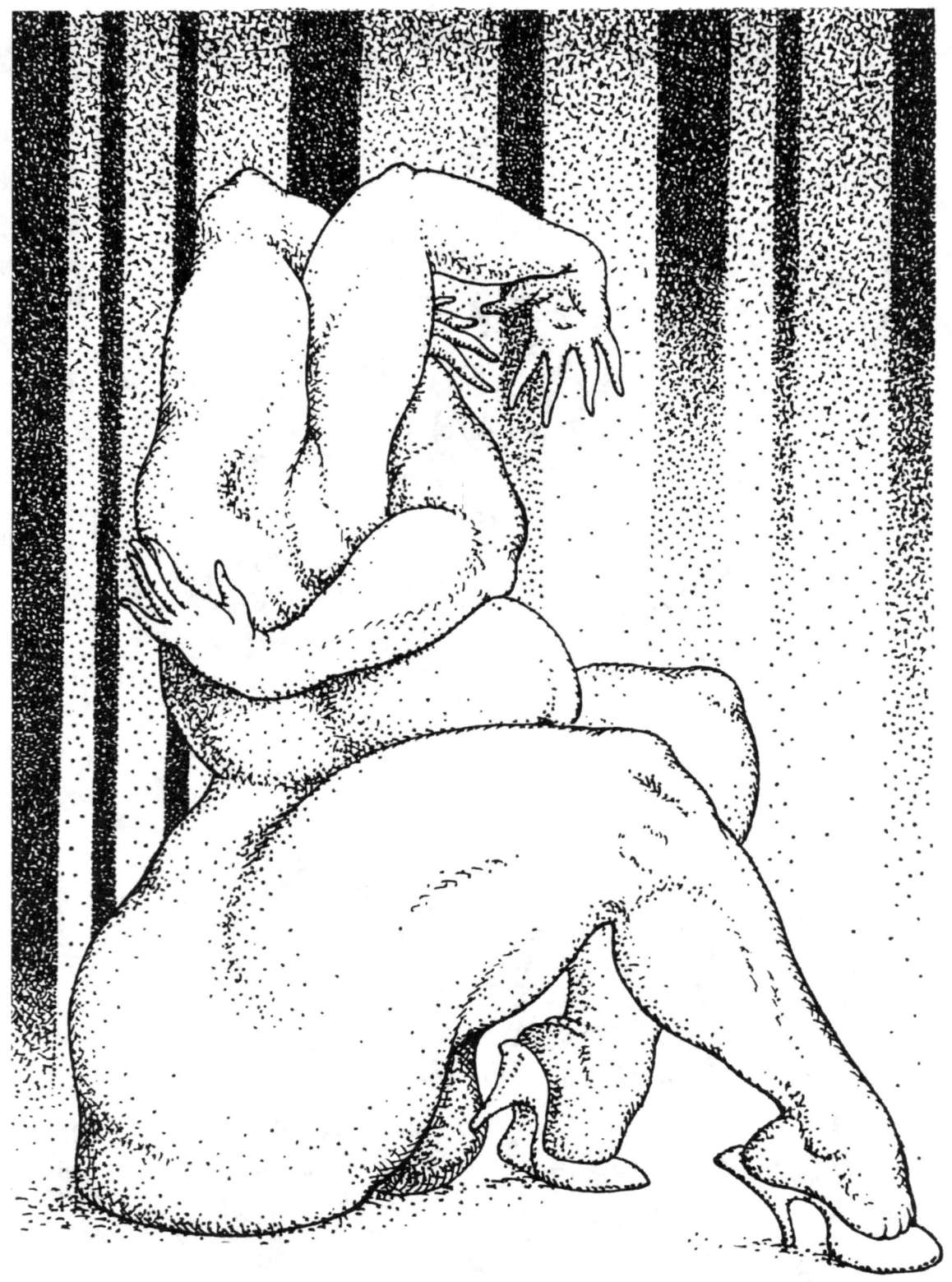

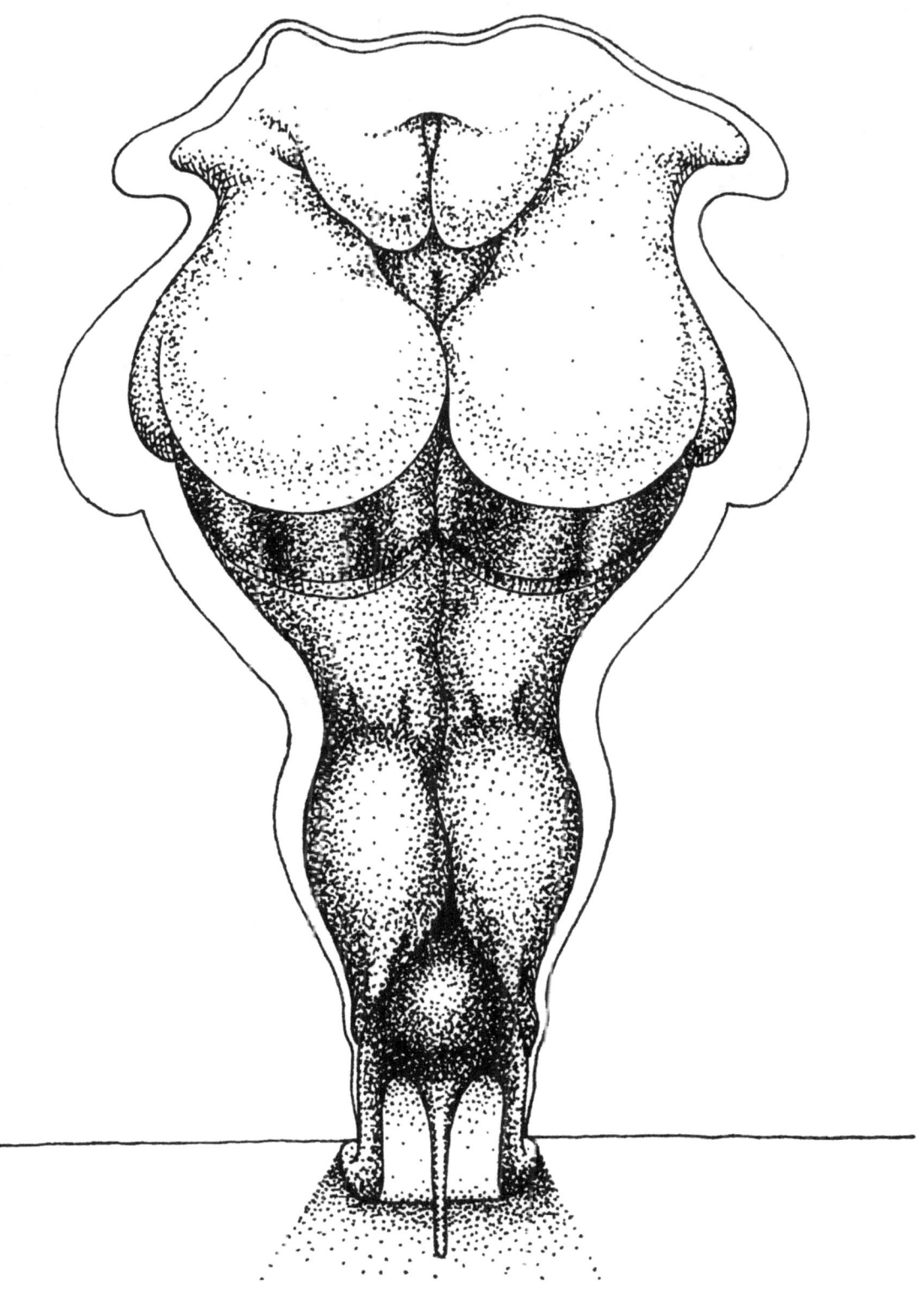

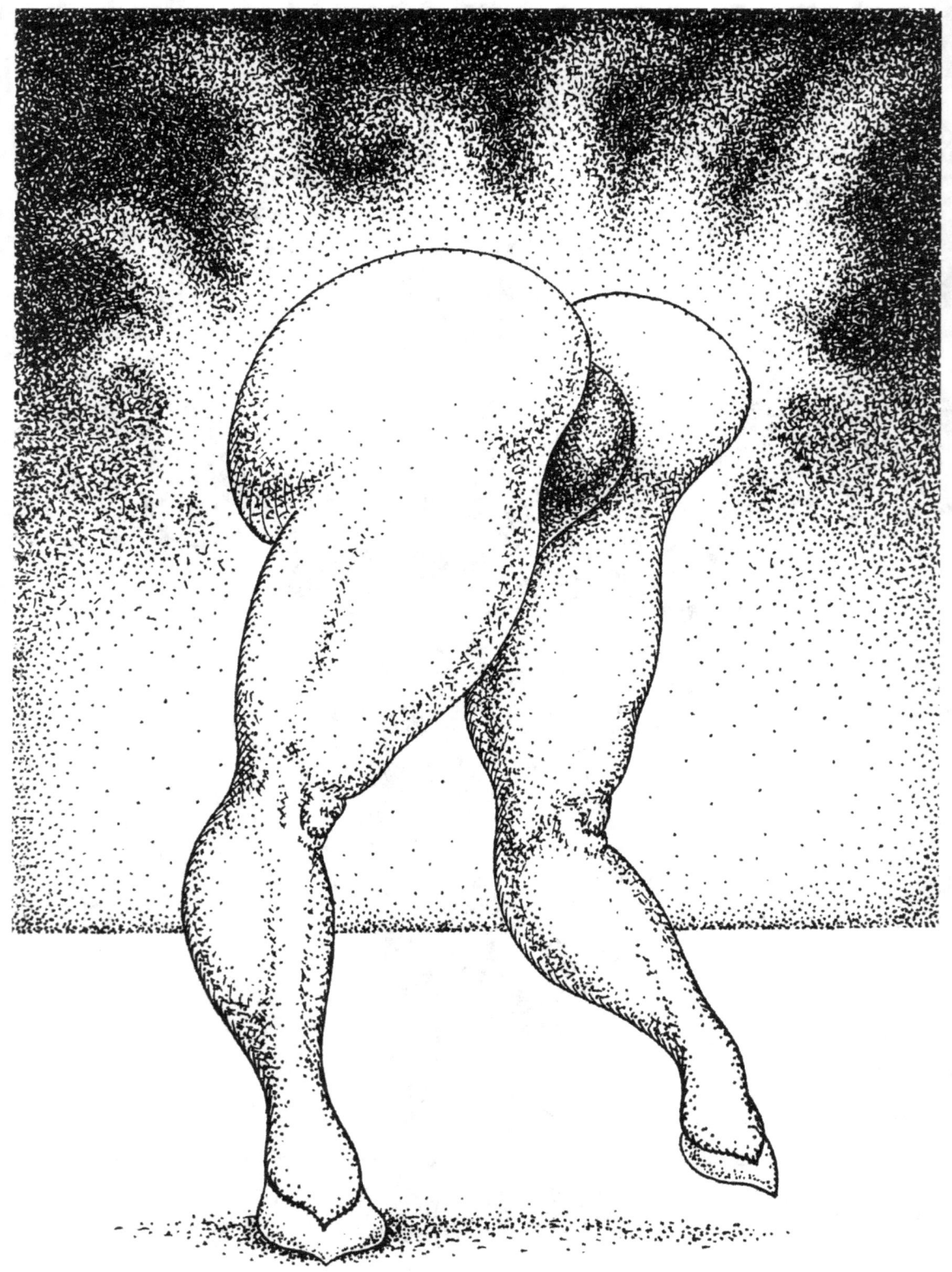

70

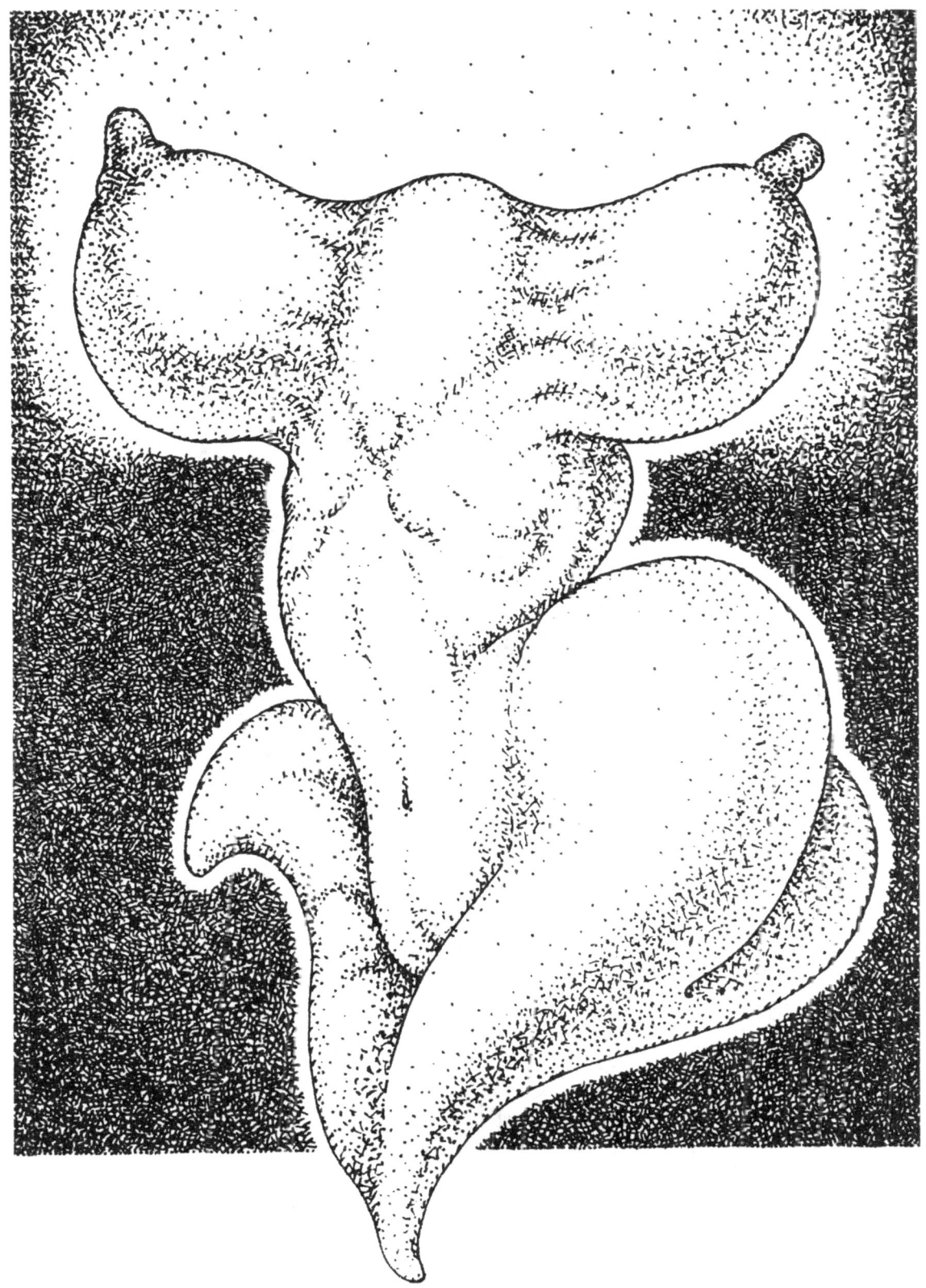

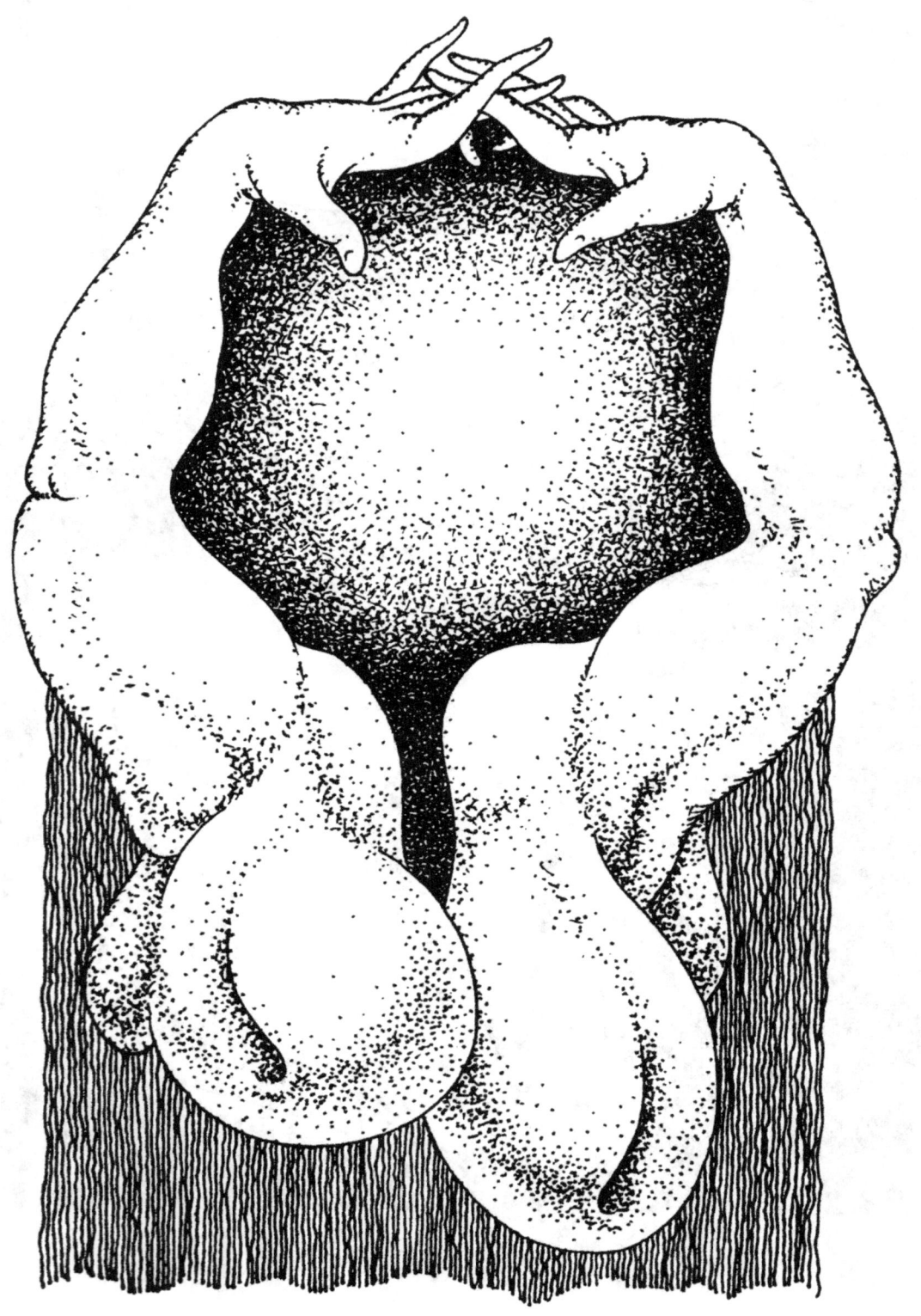

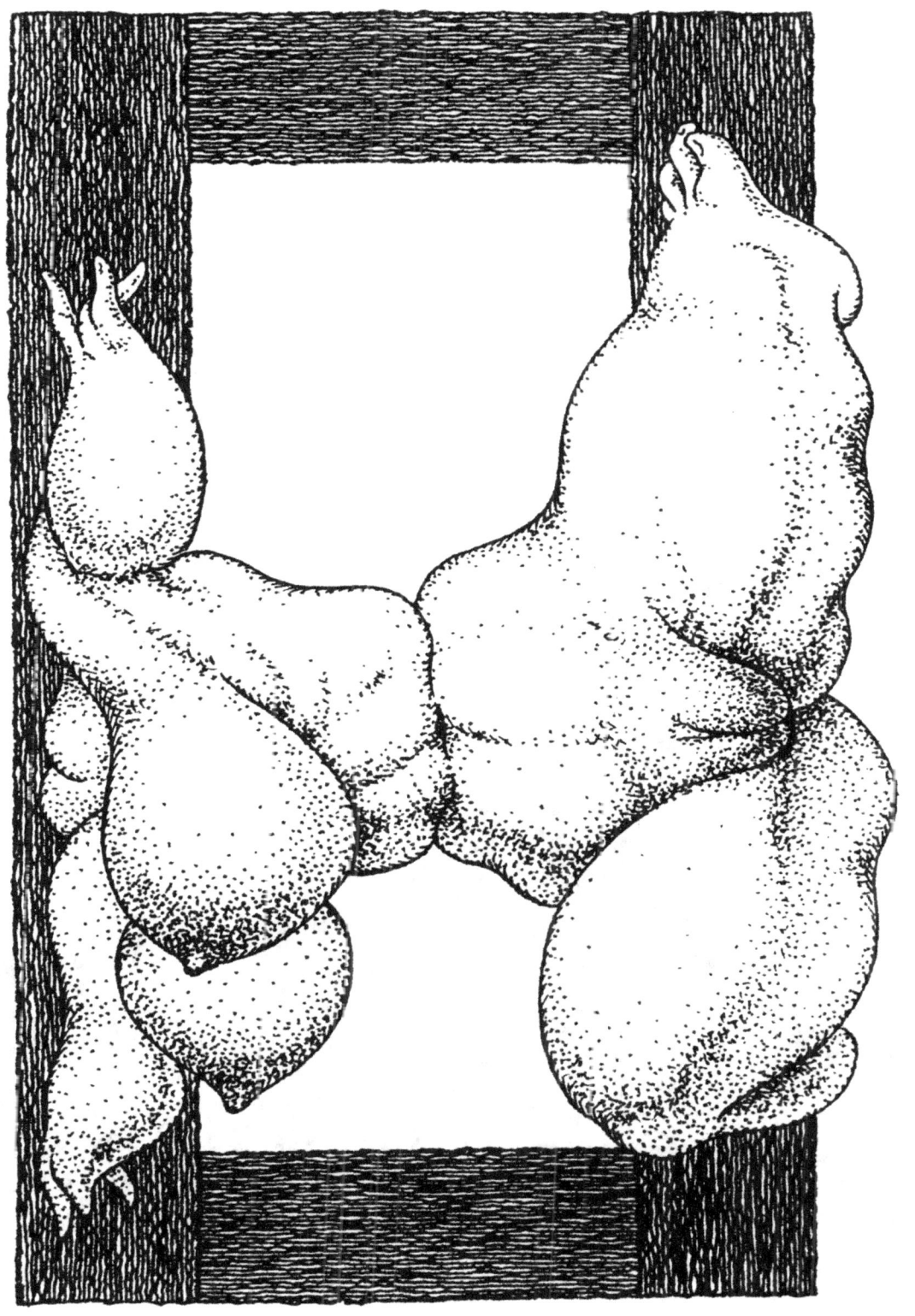

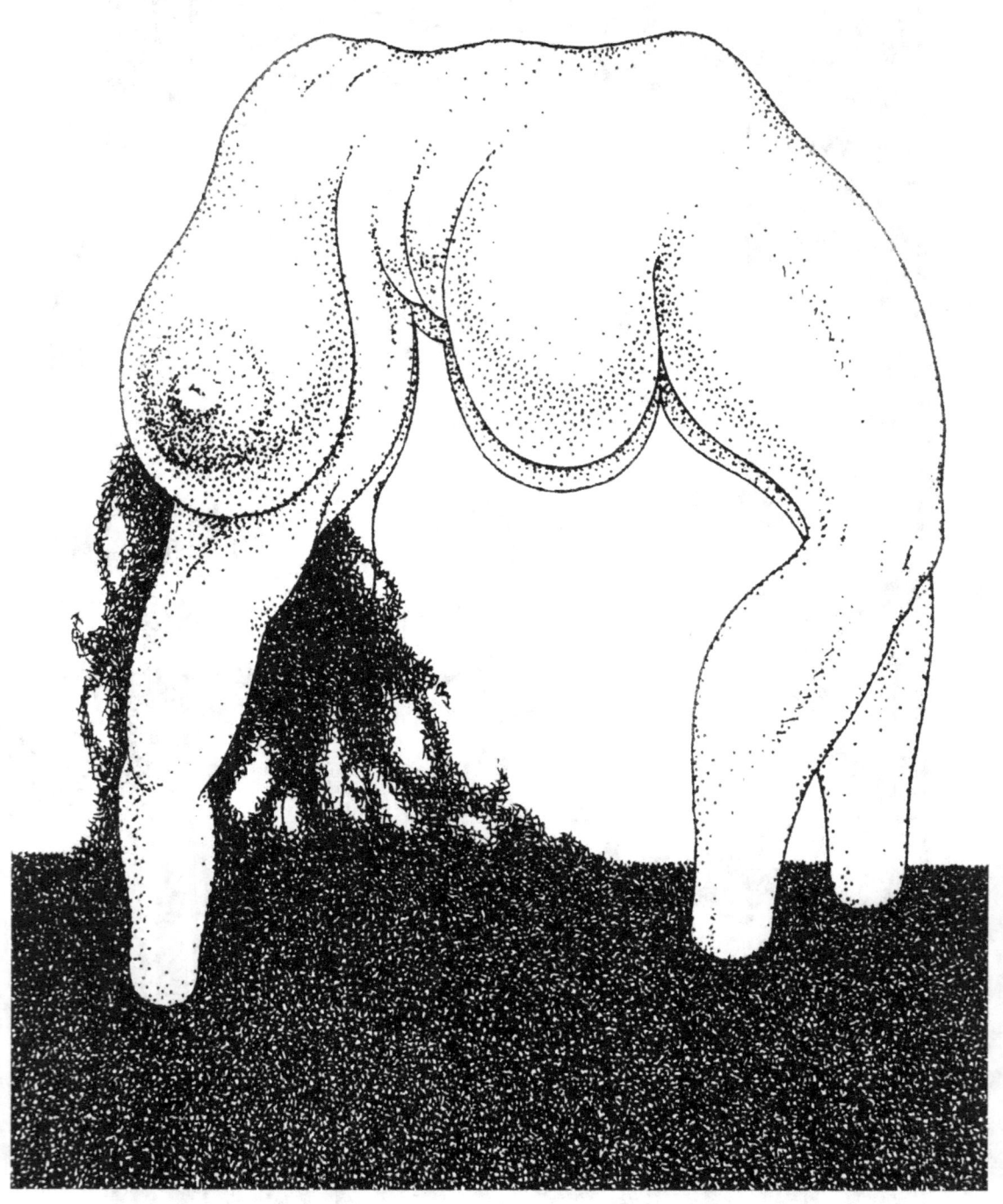

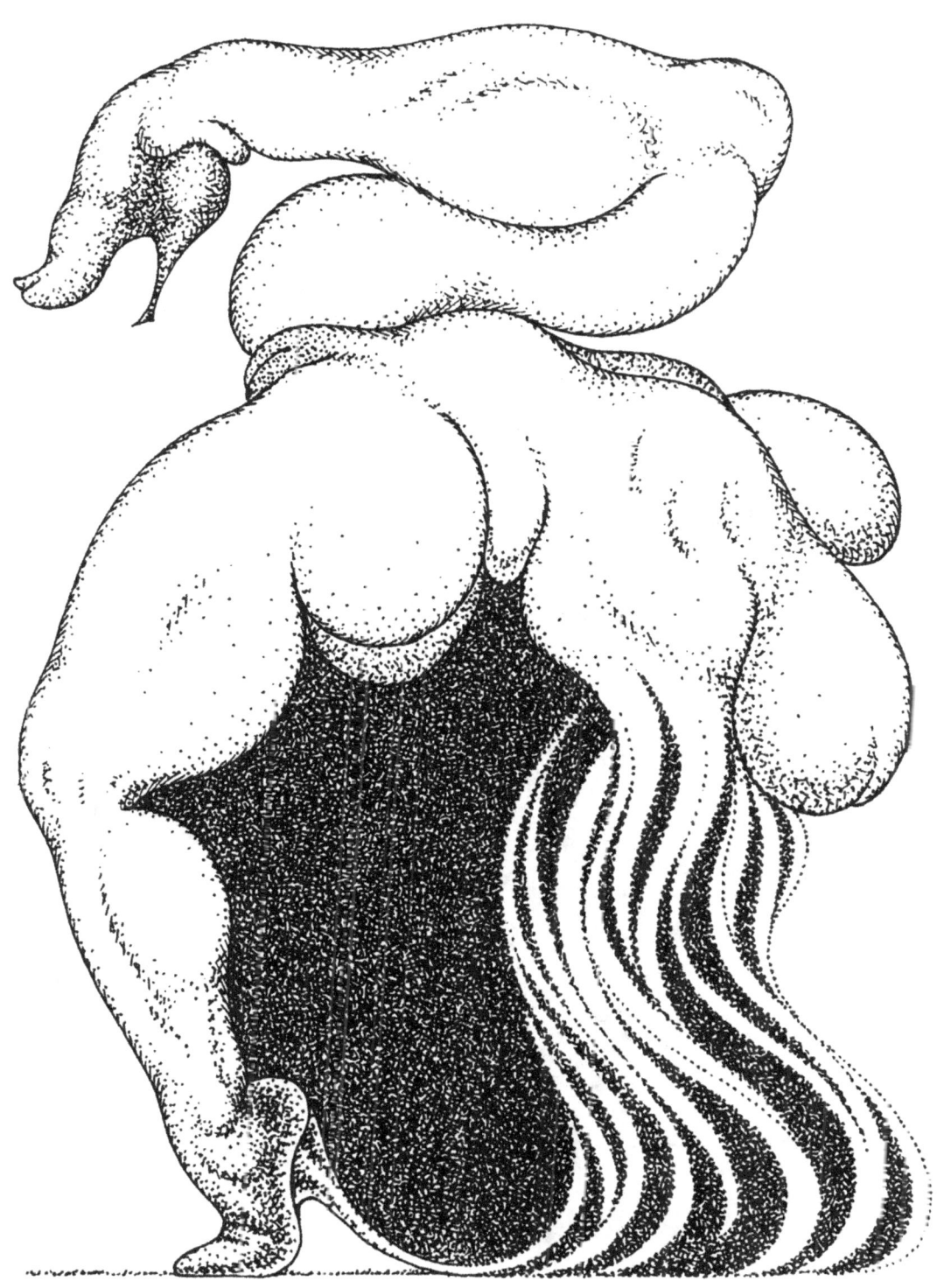

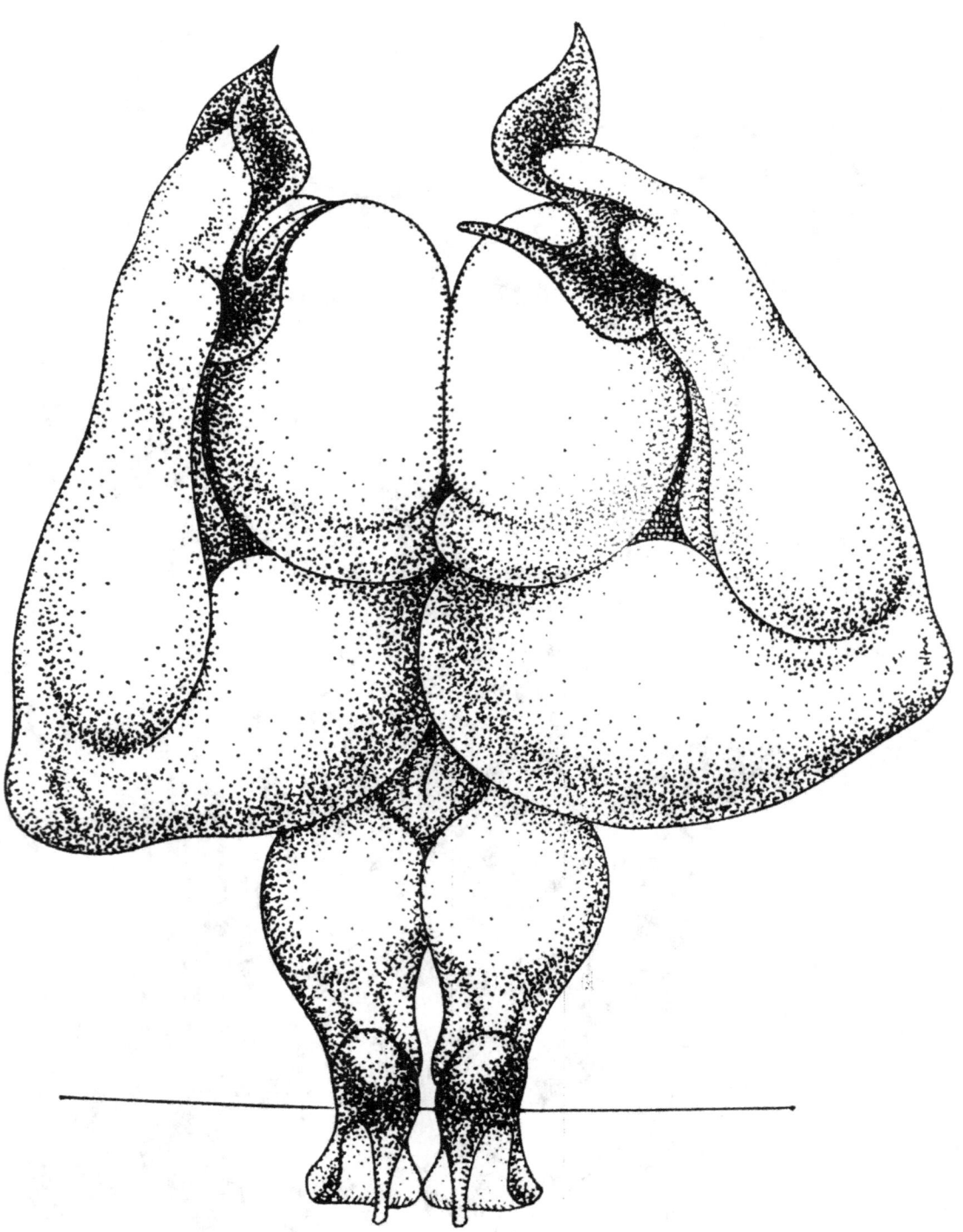

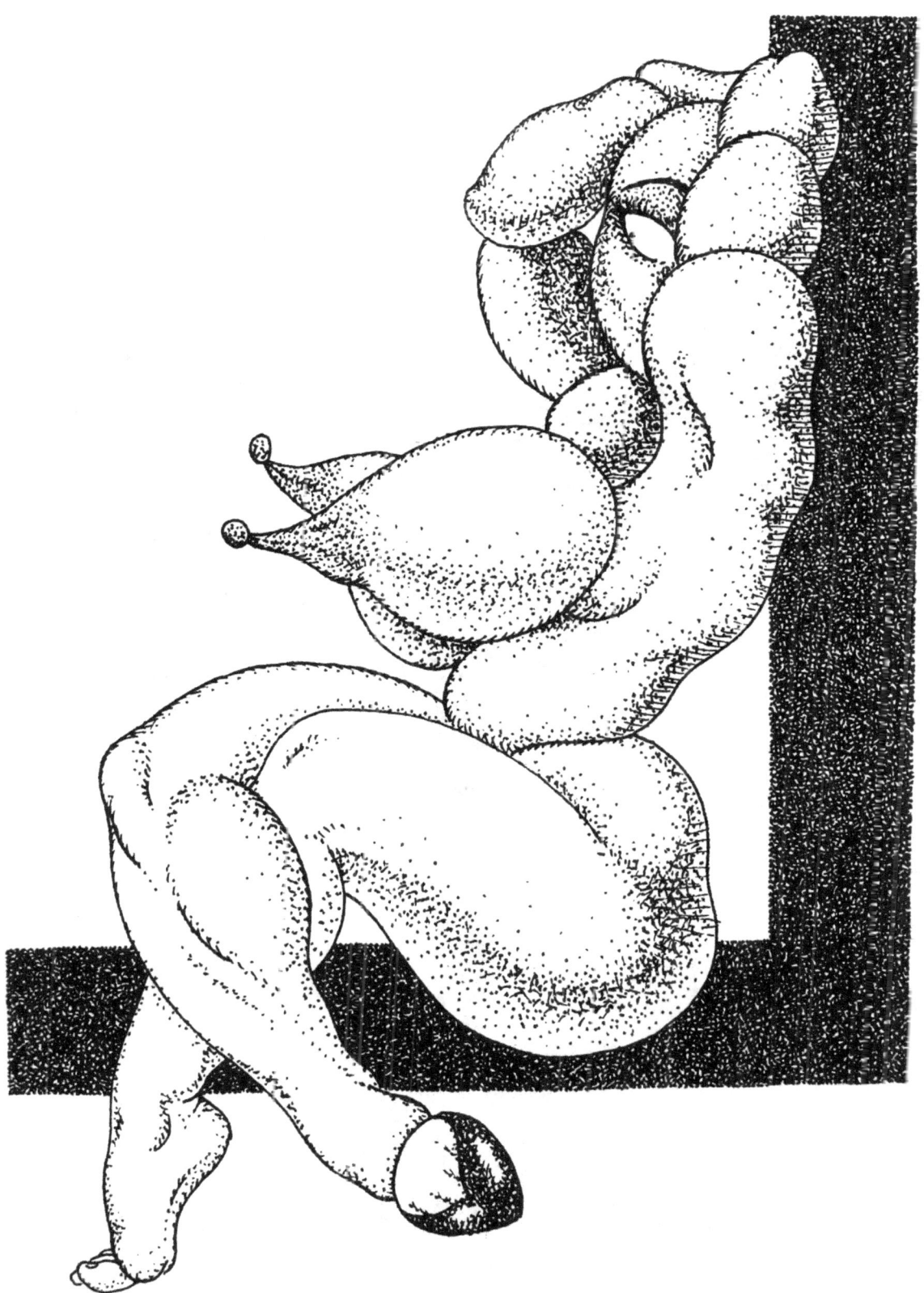

77

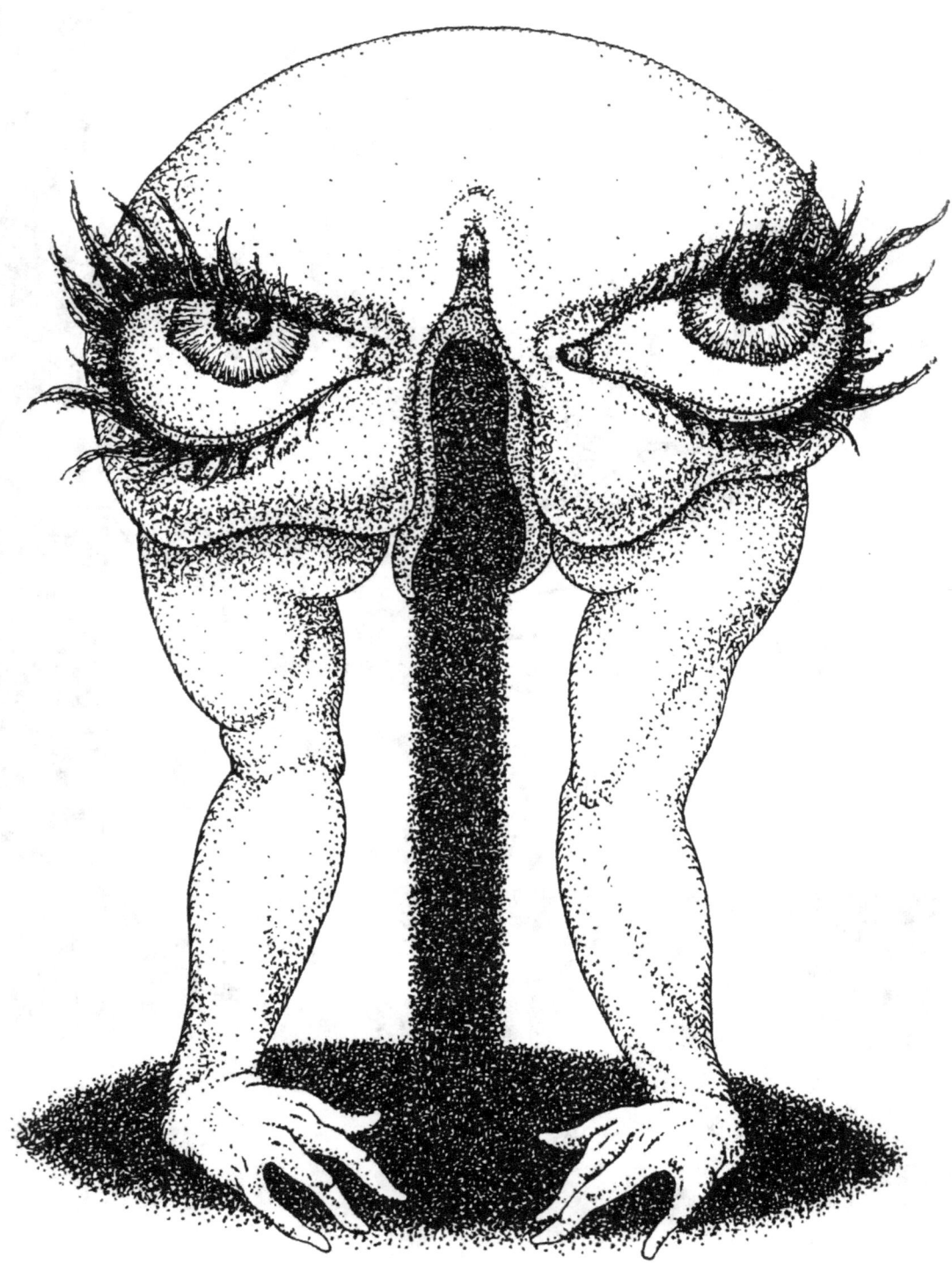

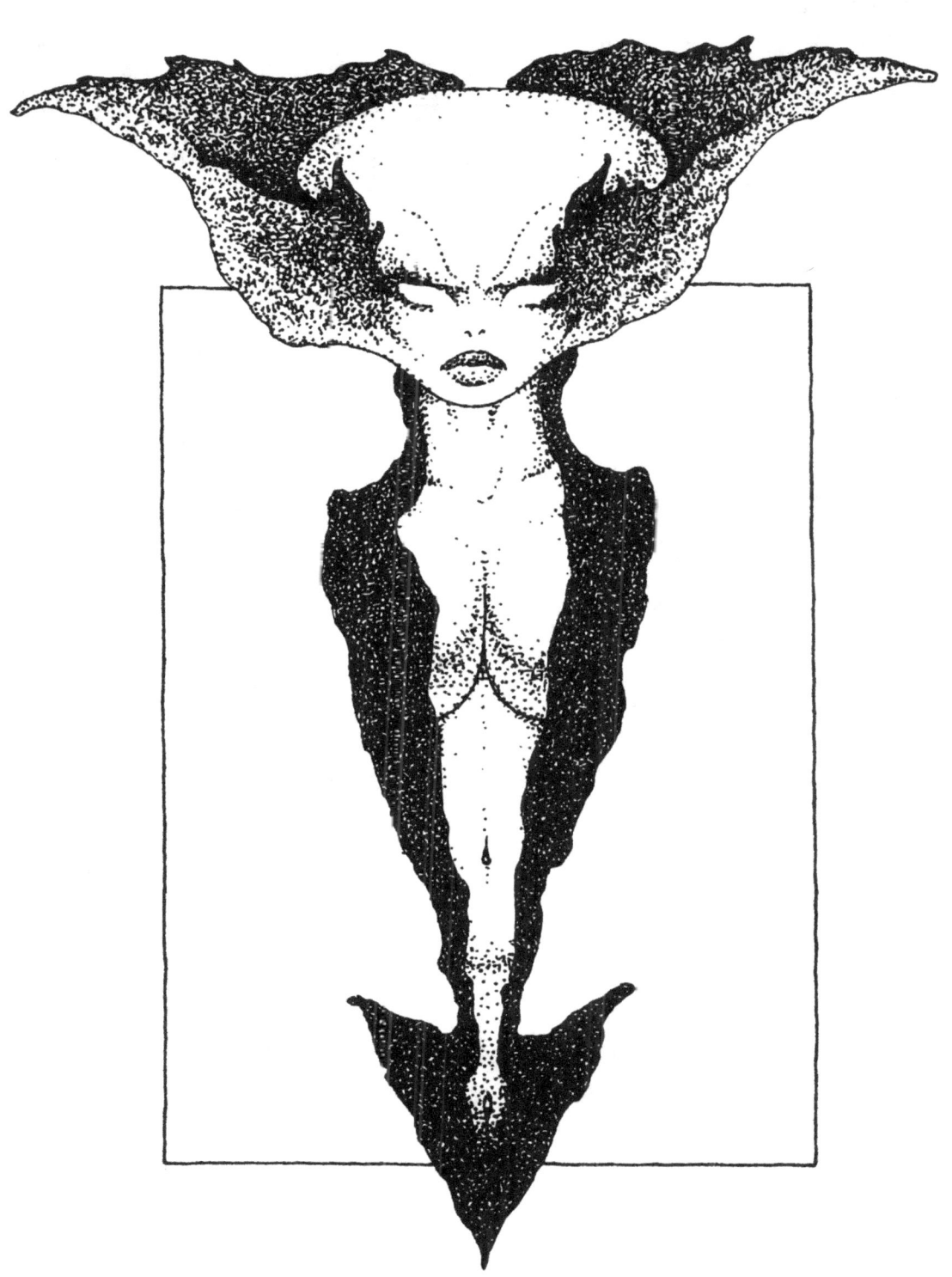

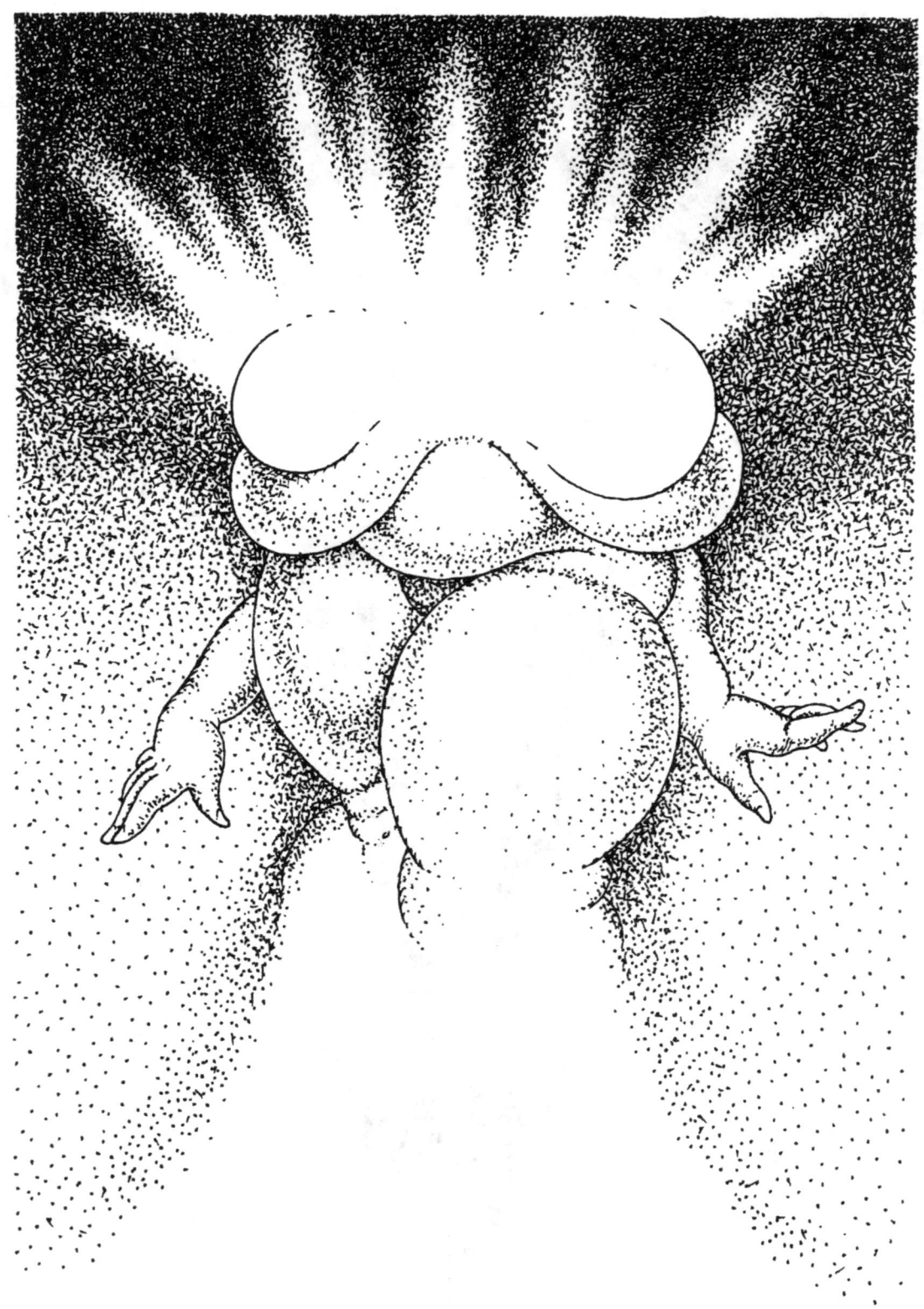

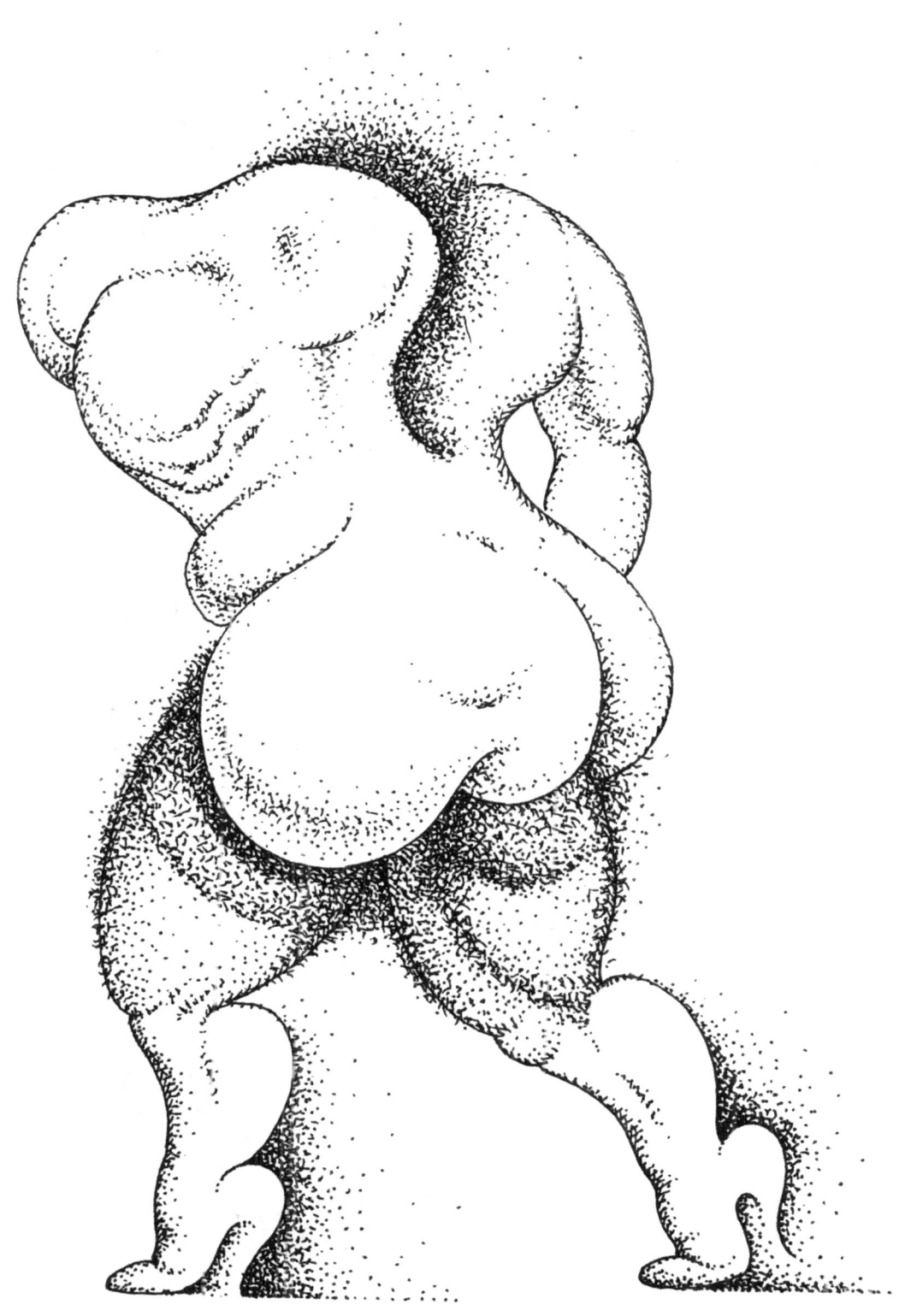

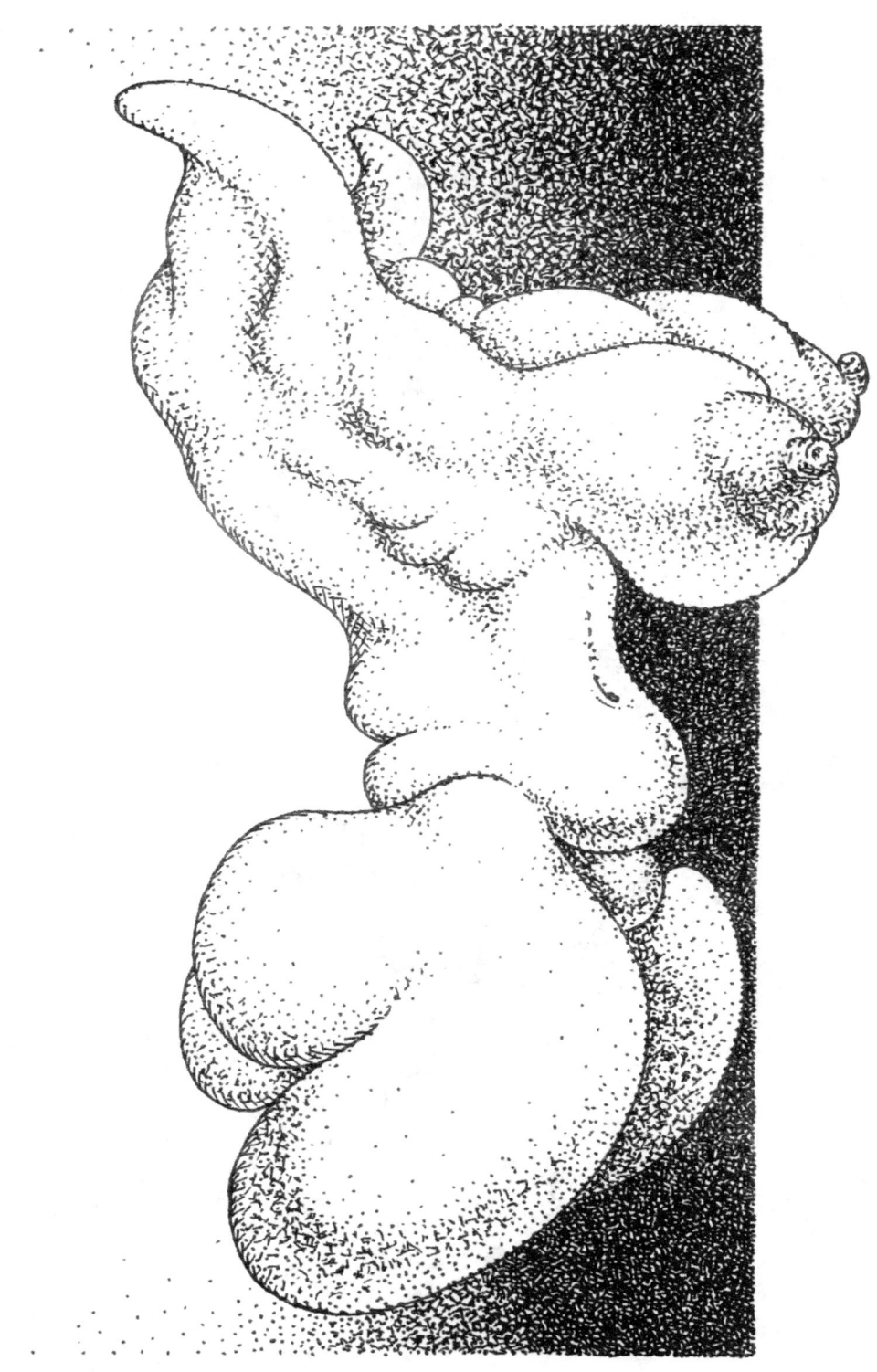

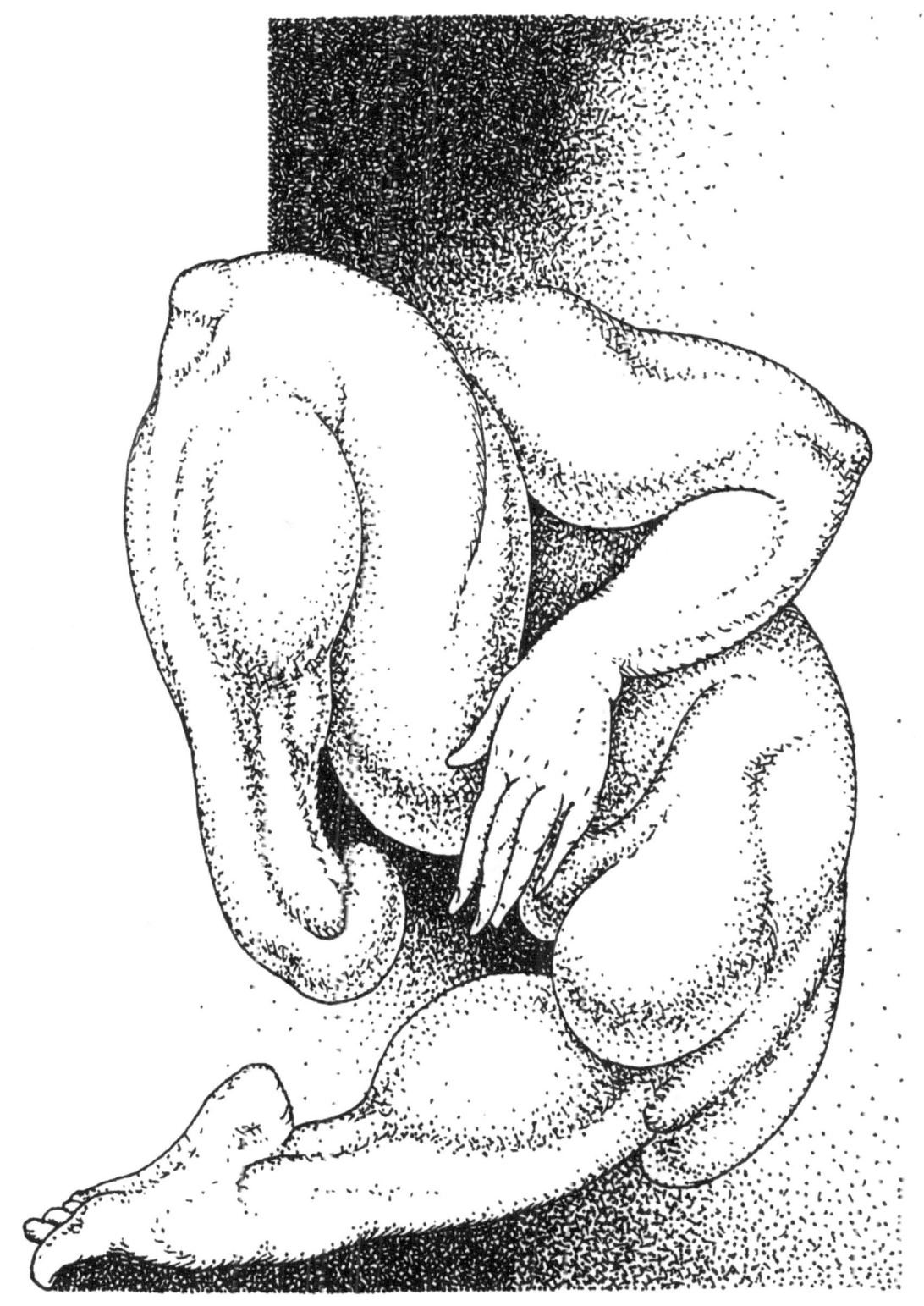

83

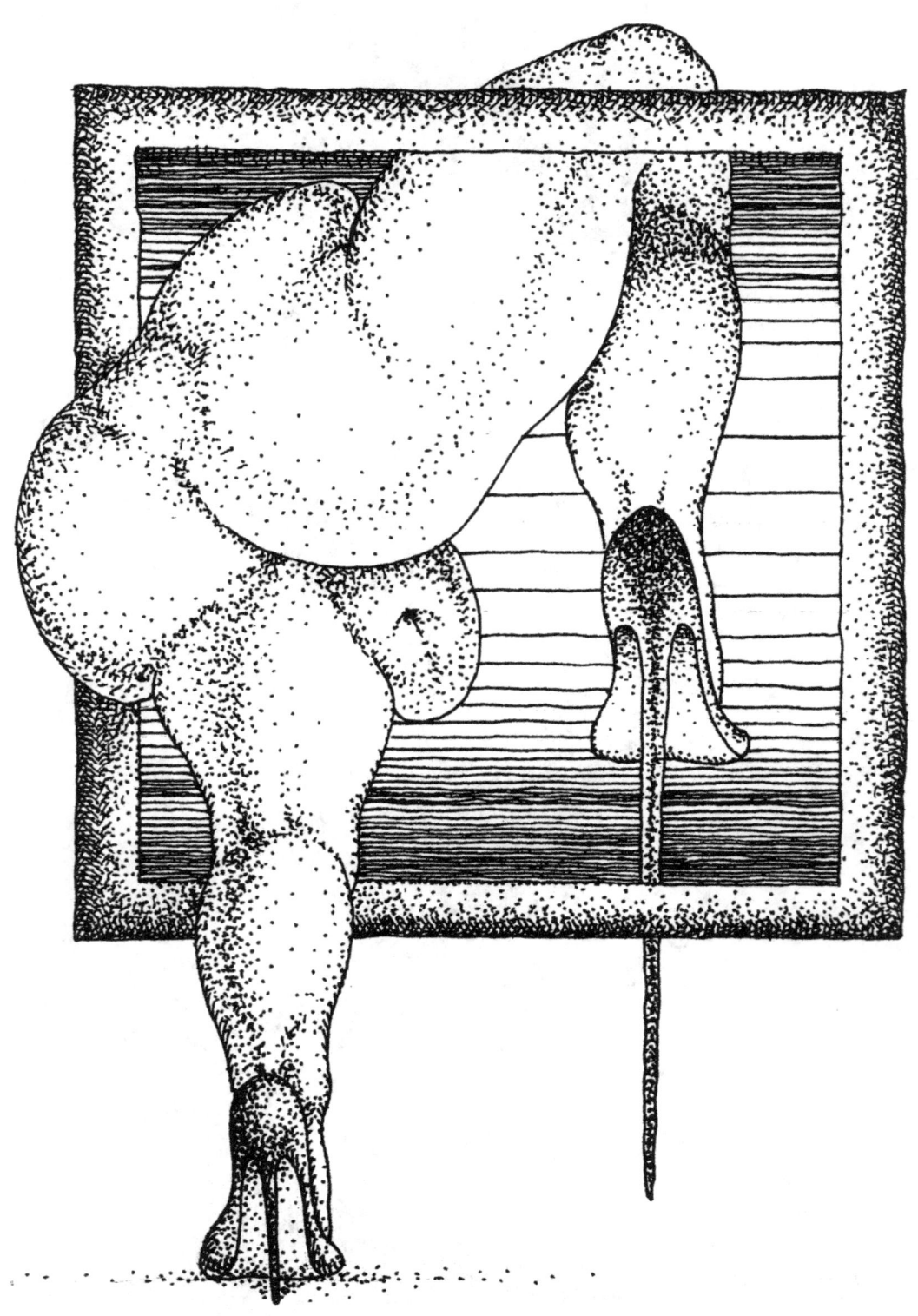

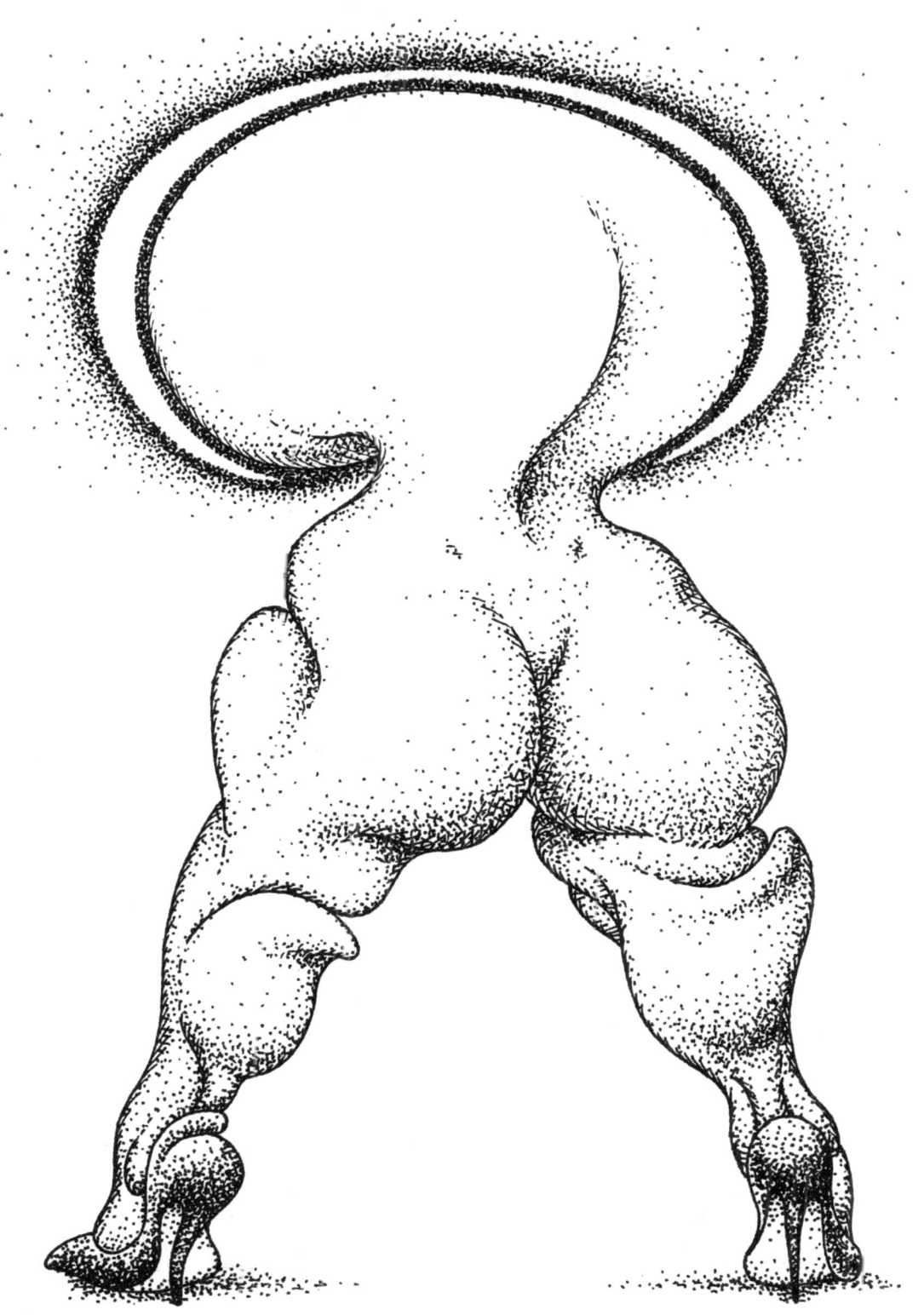

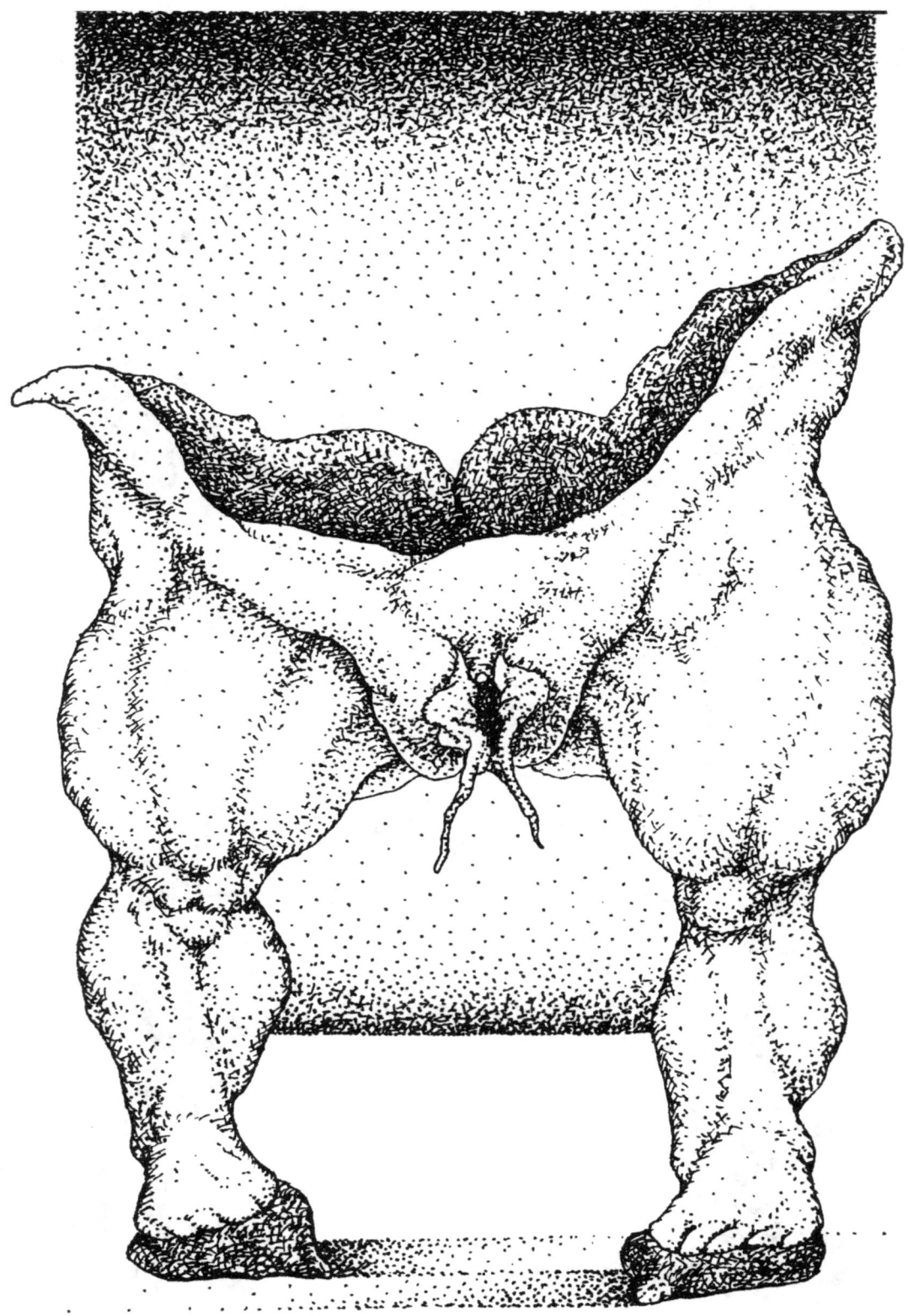

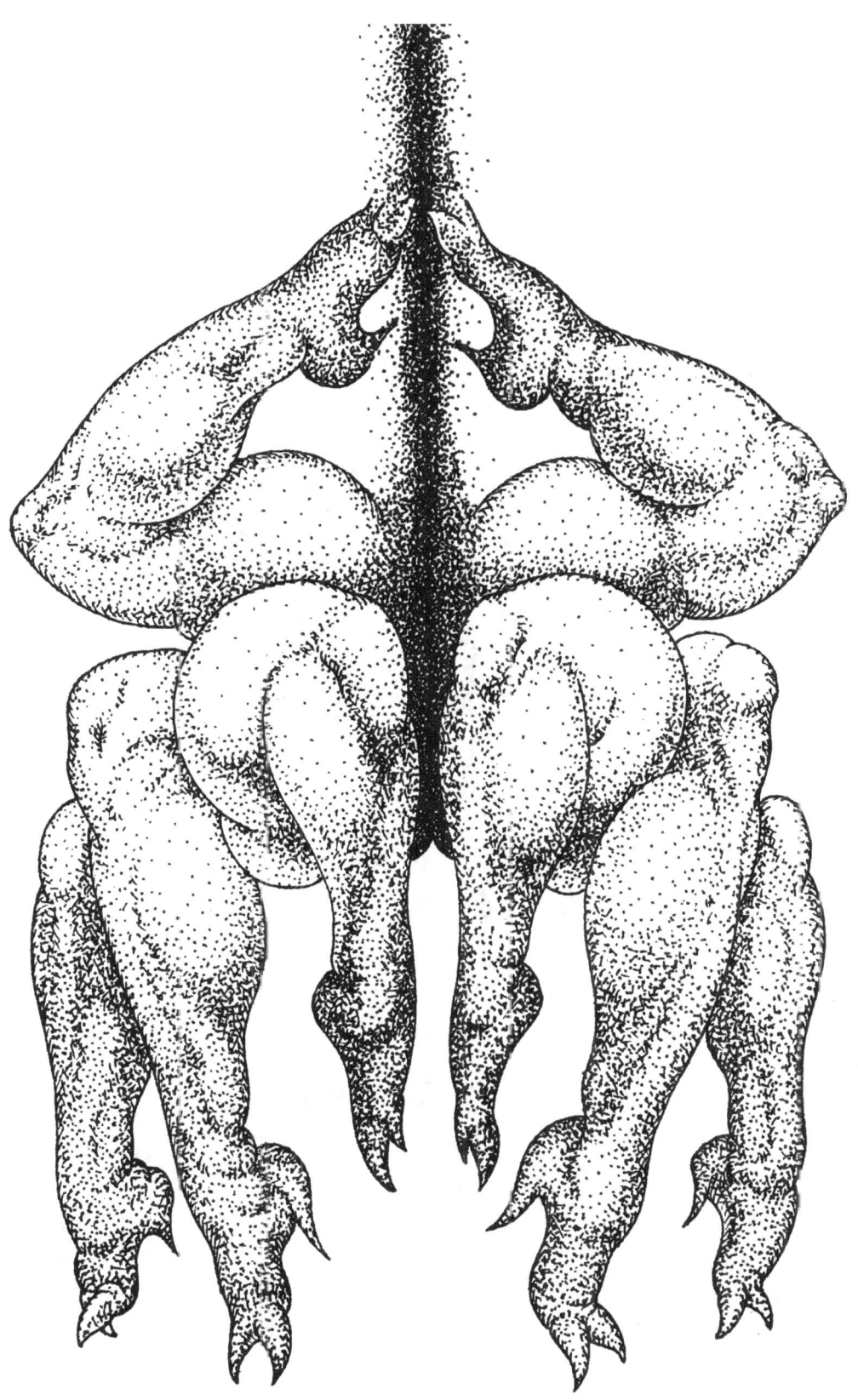

87

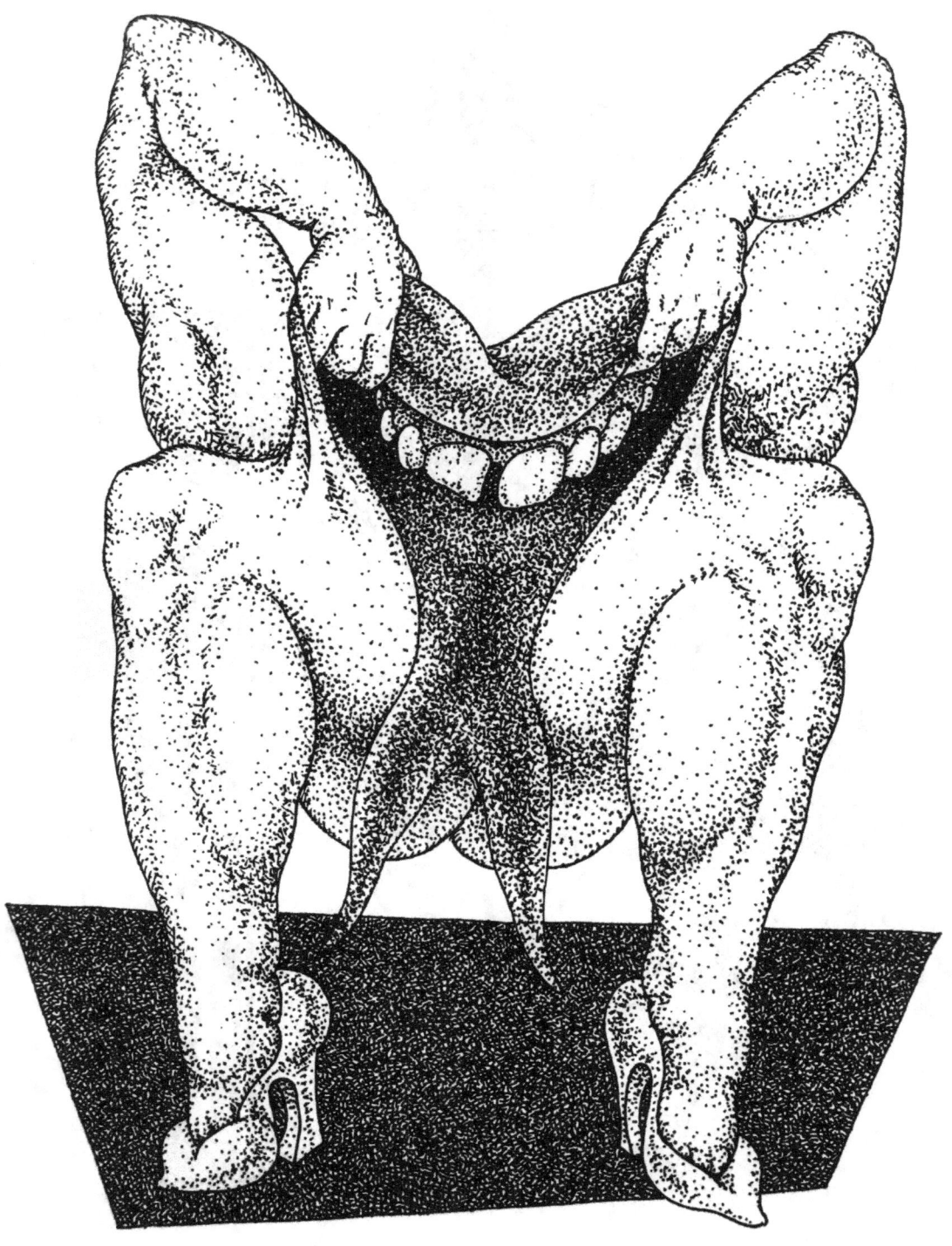

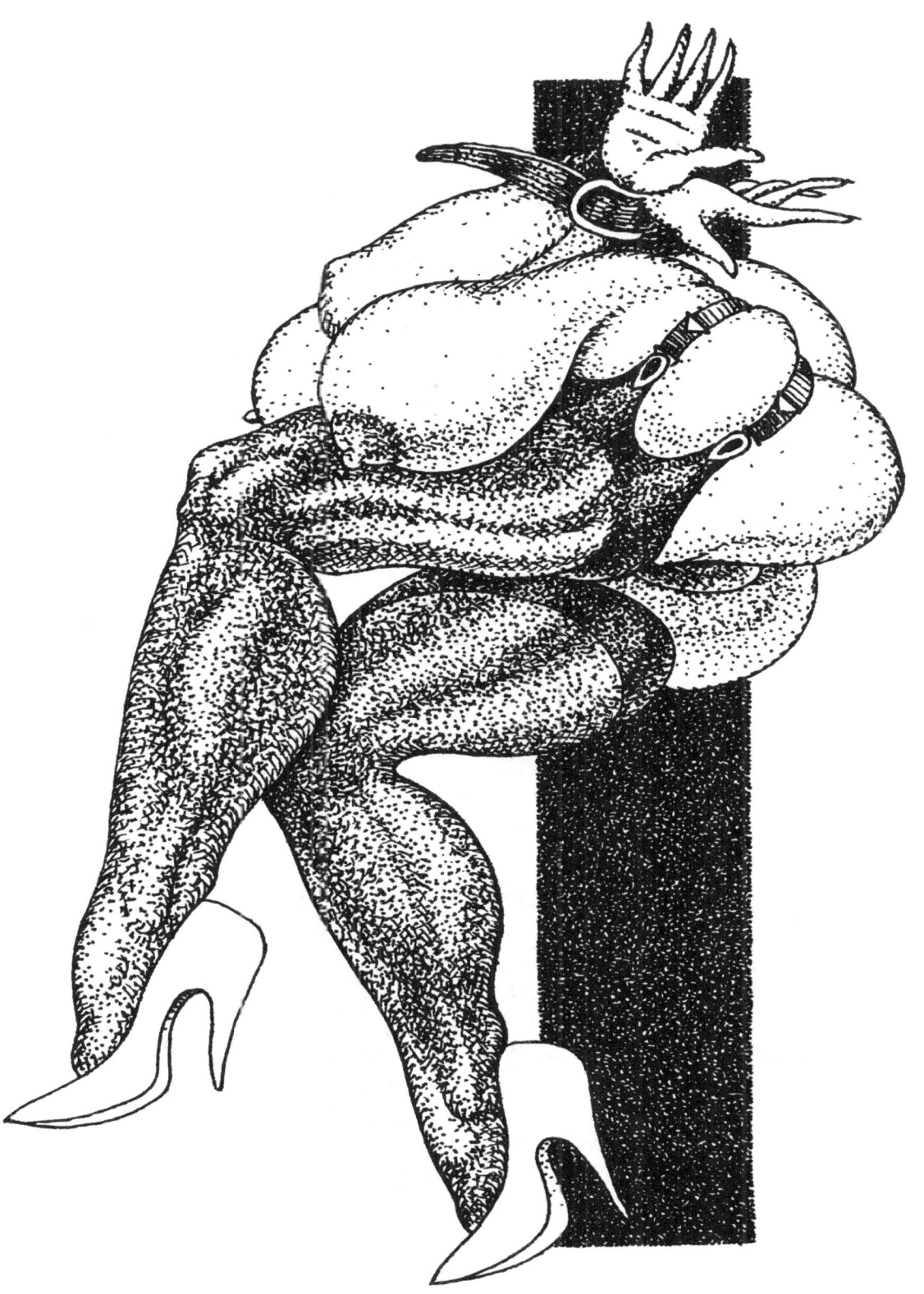

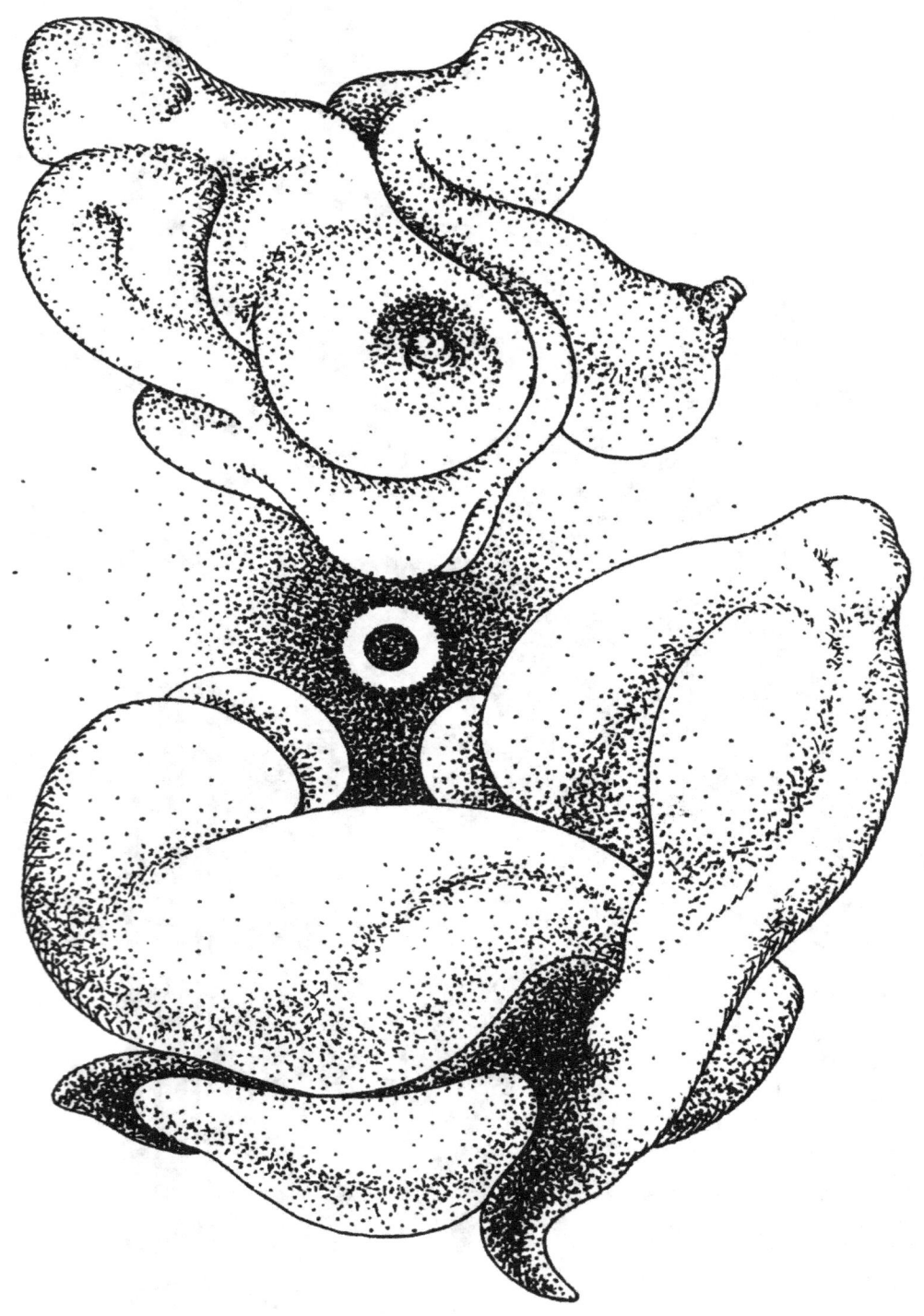

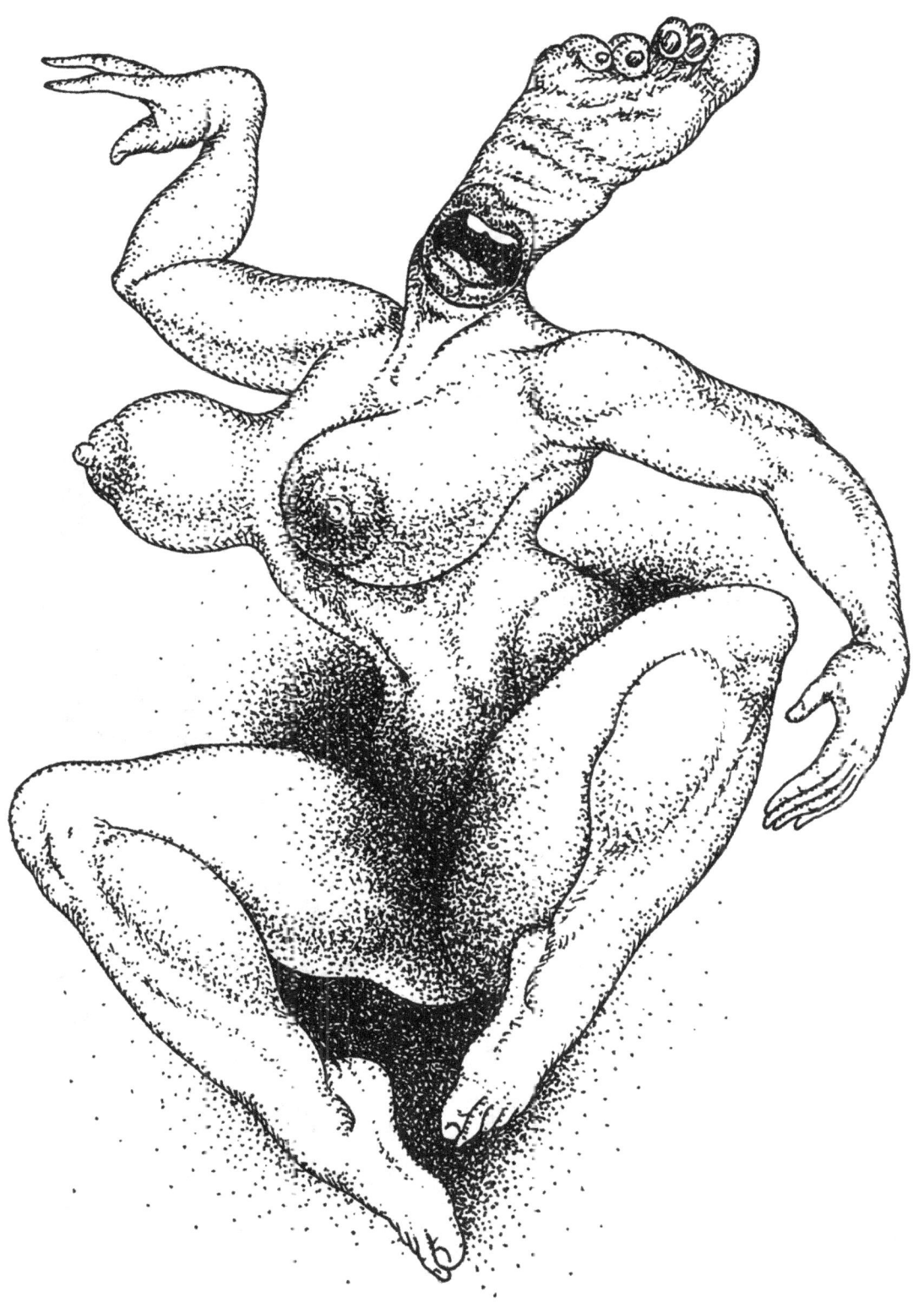

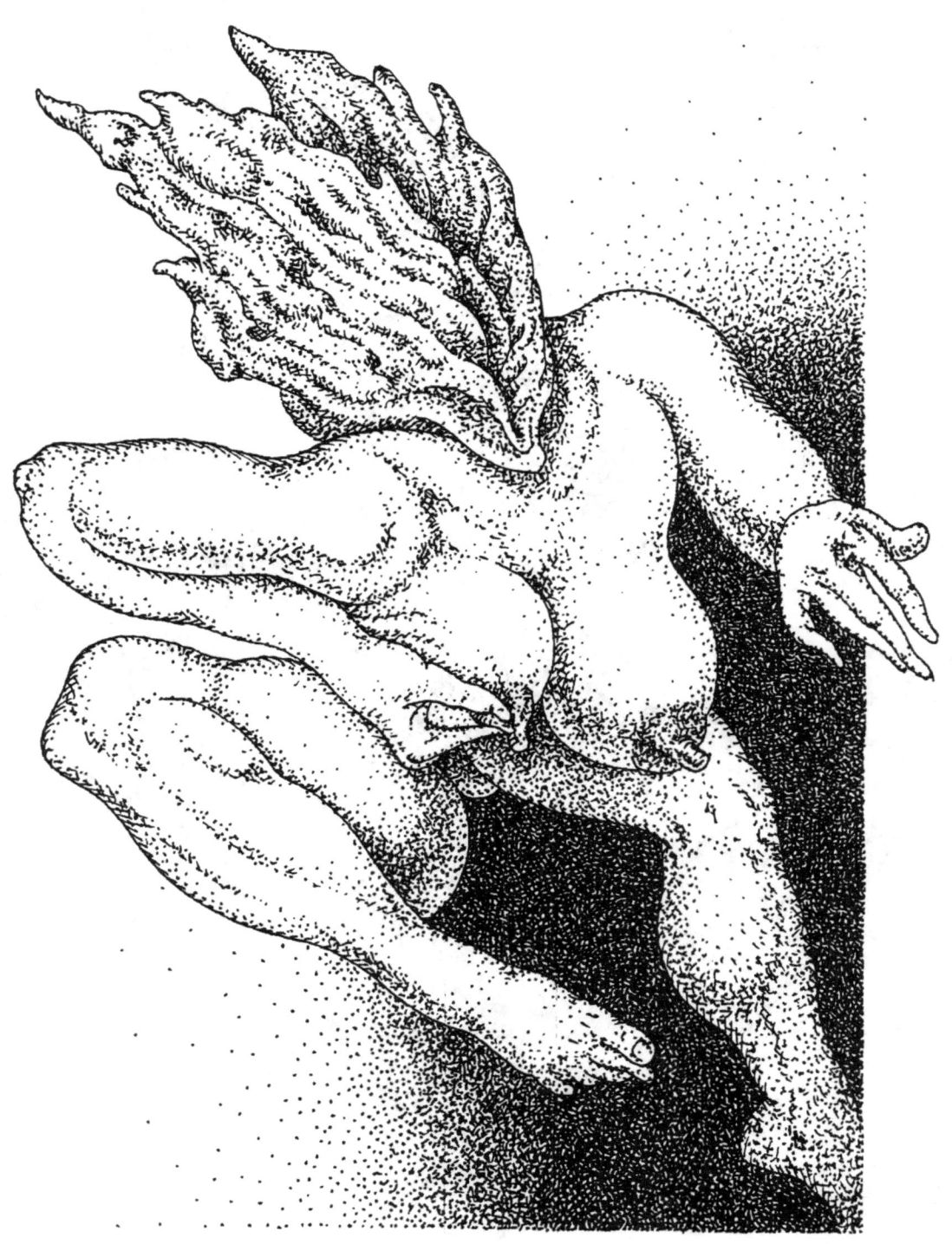

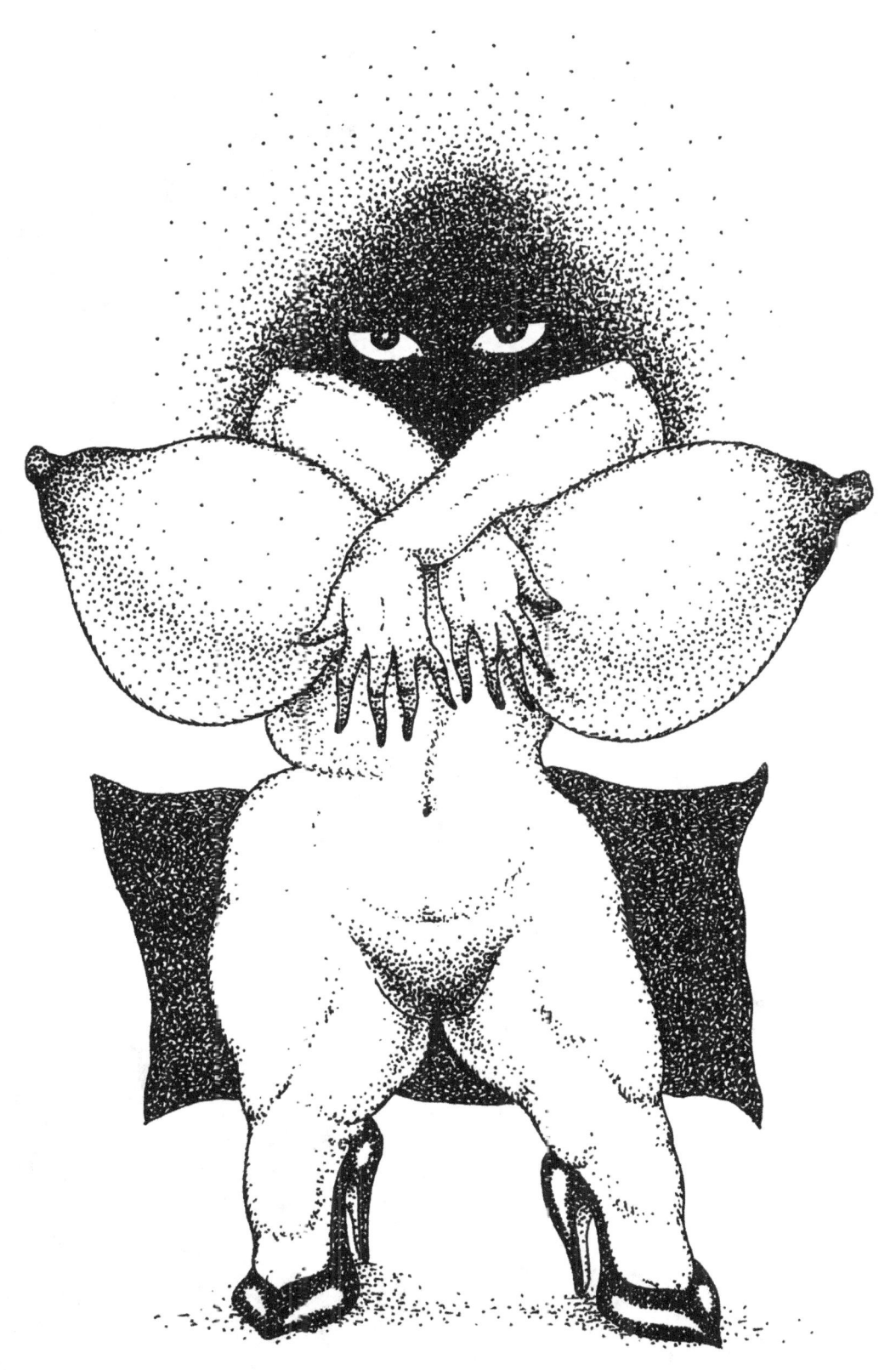

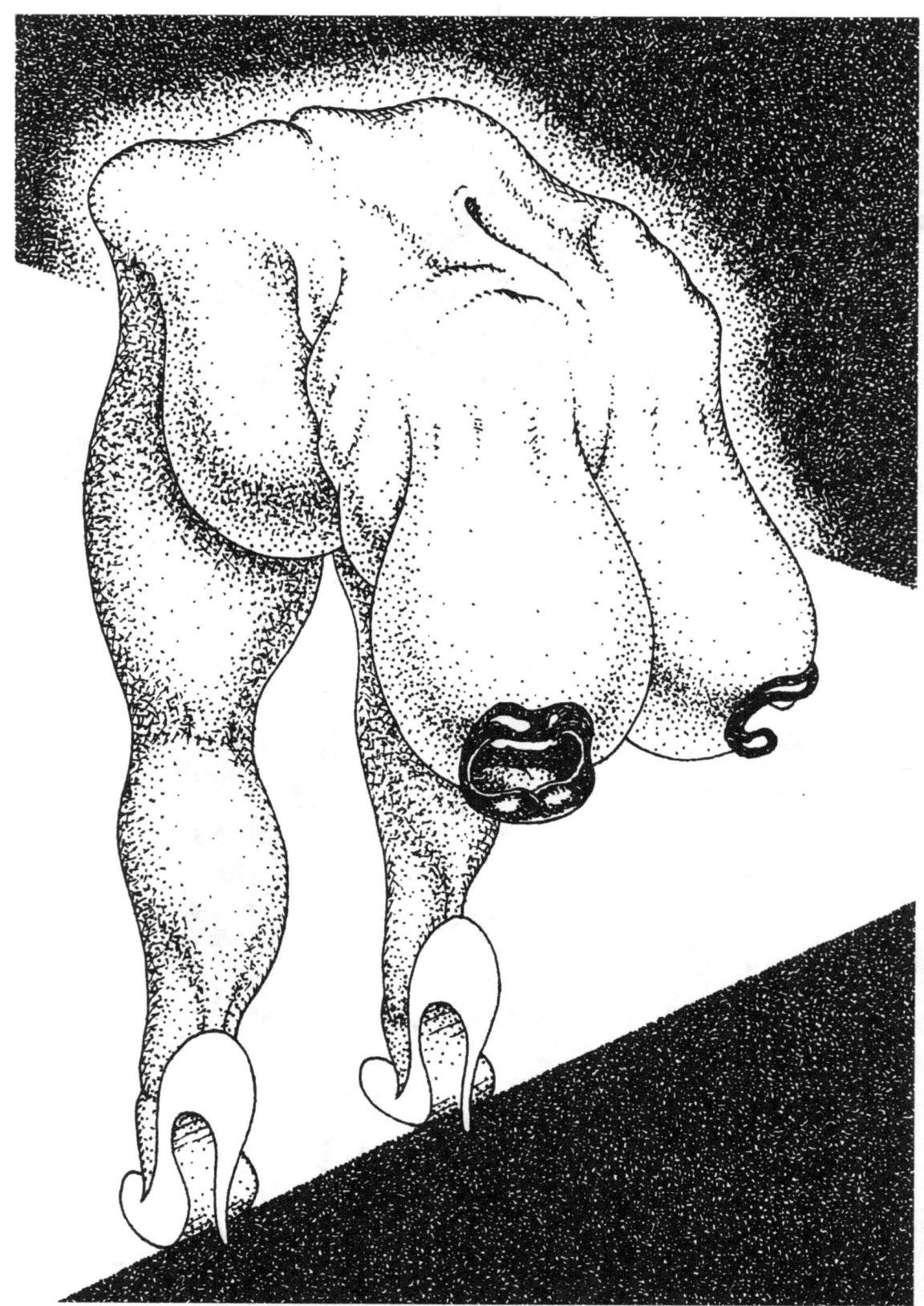

94

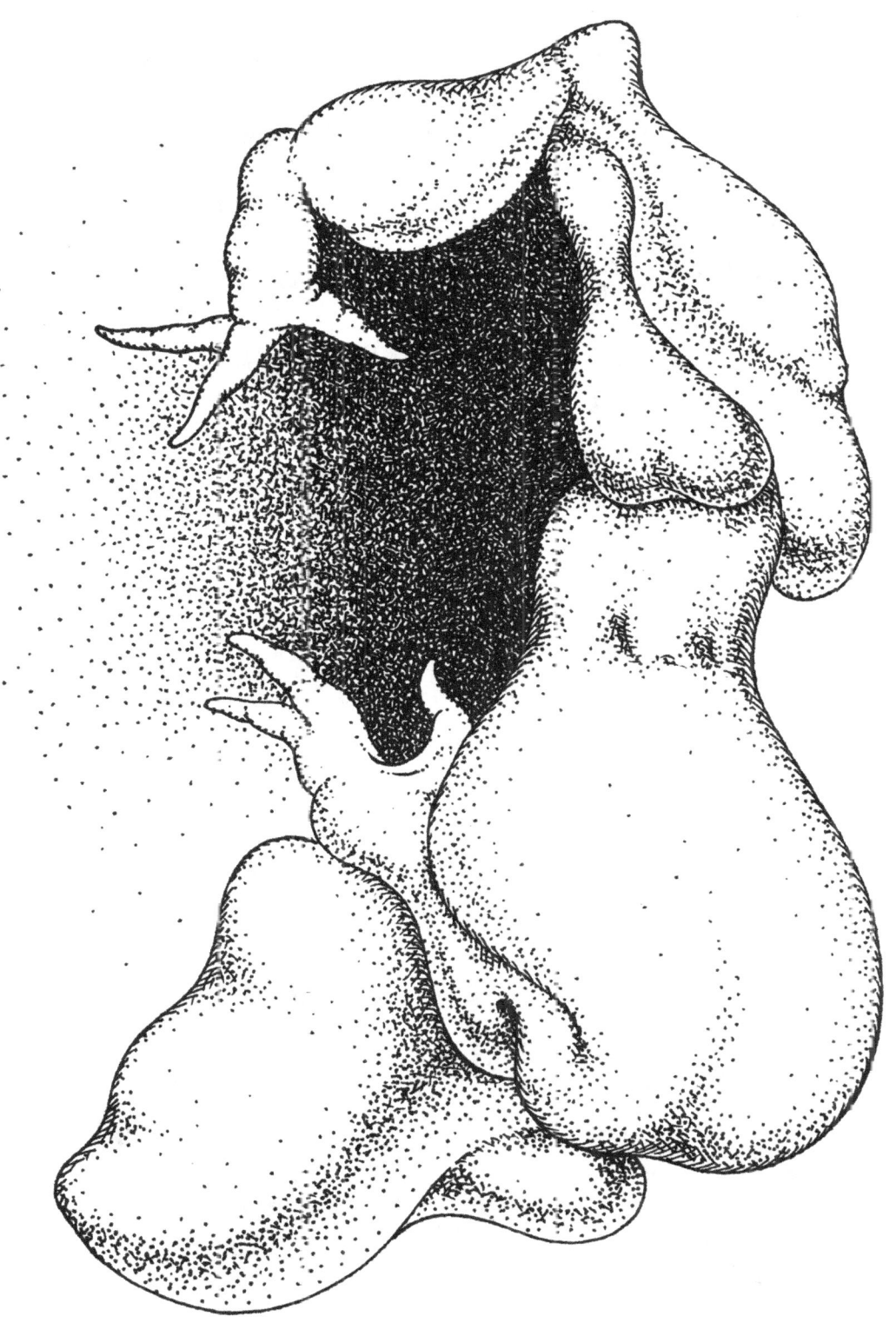

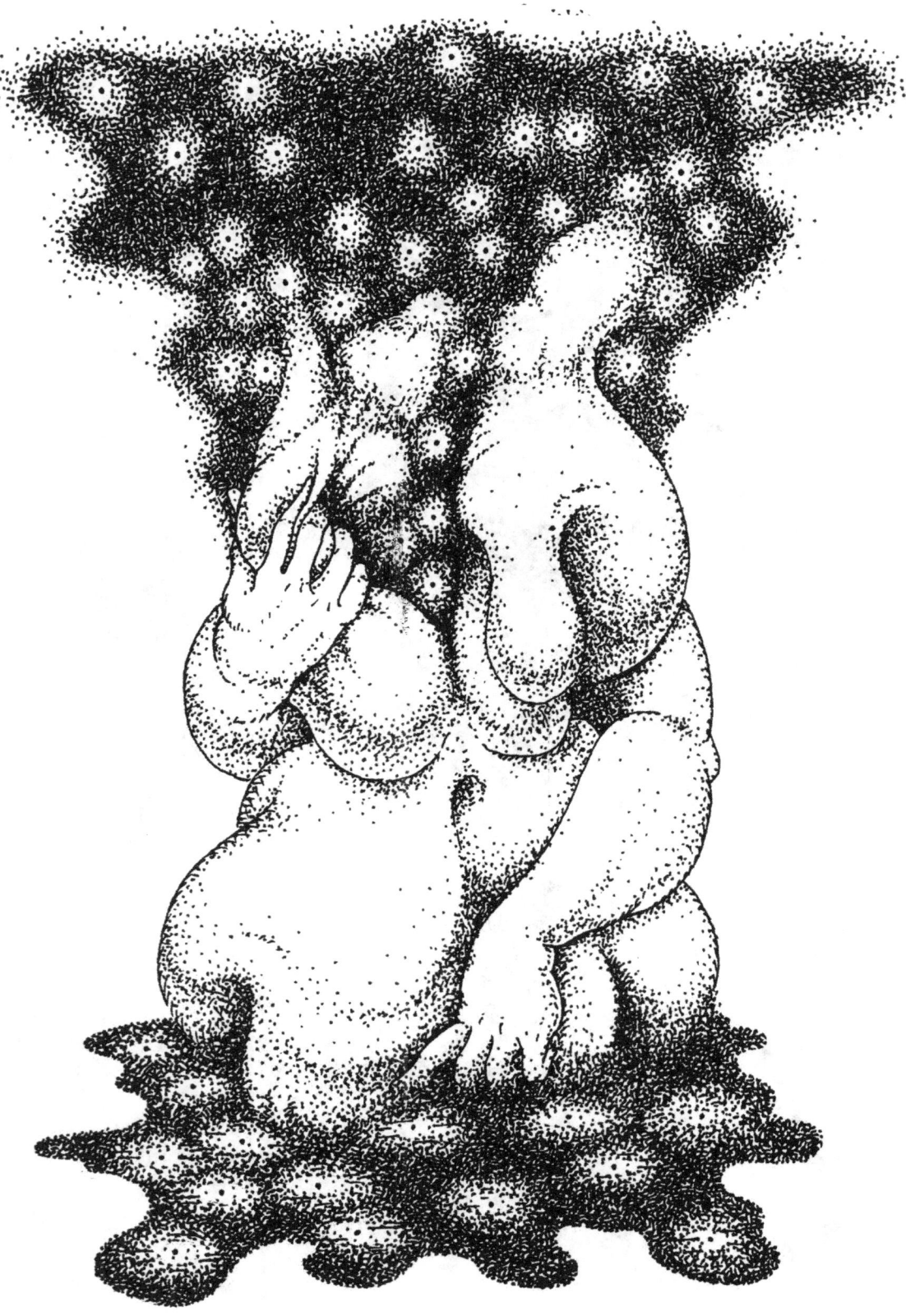

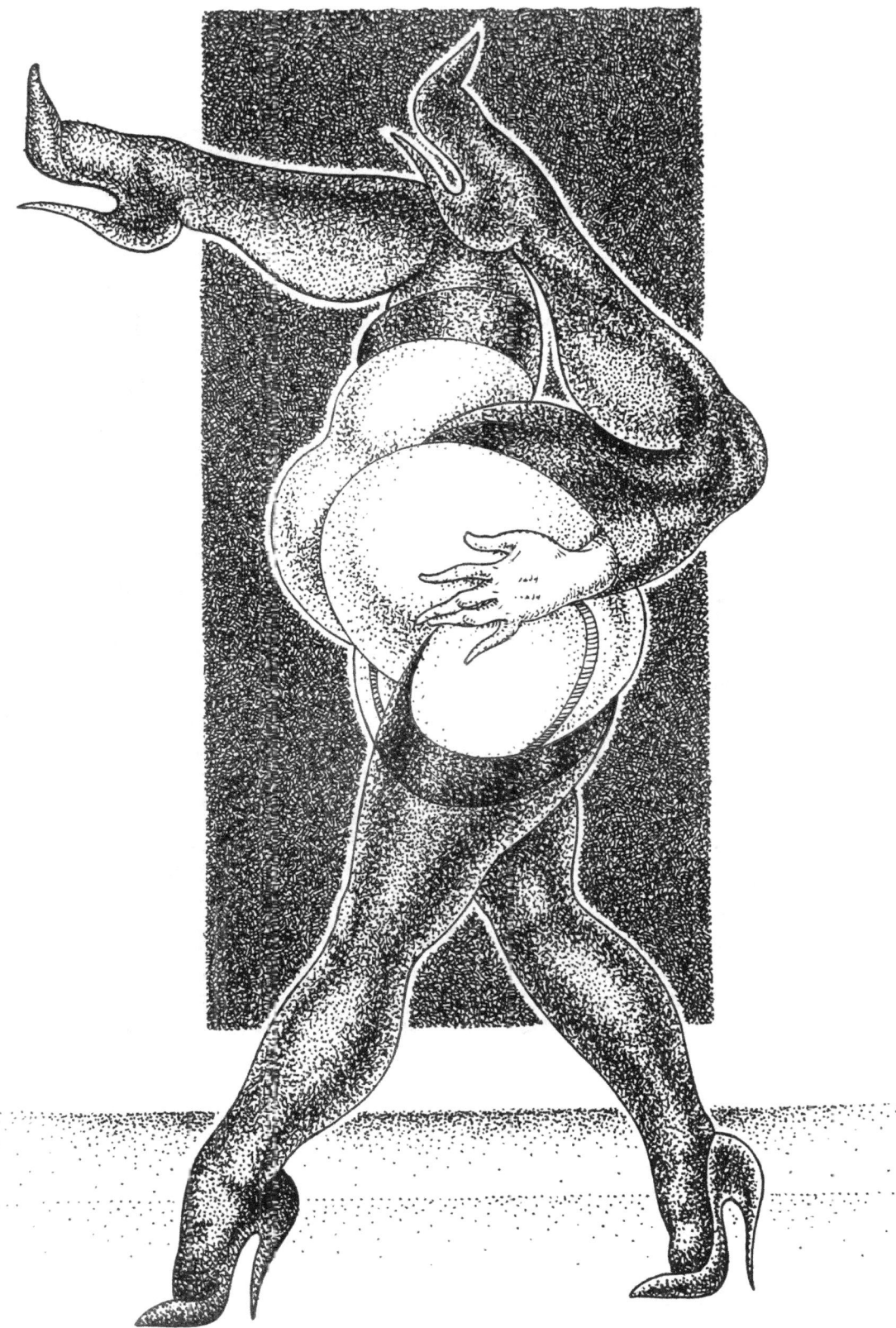

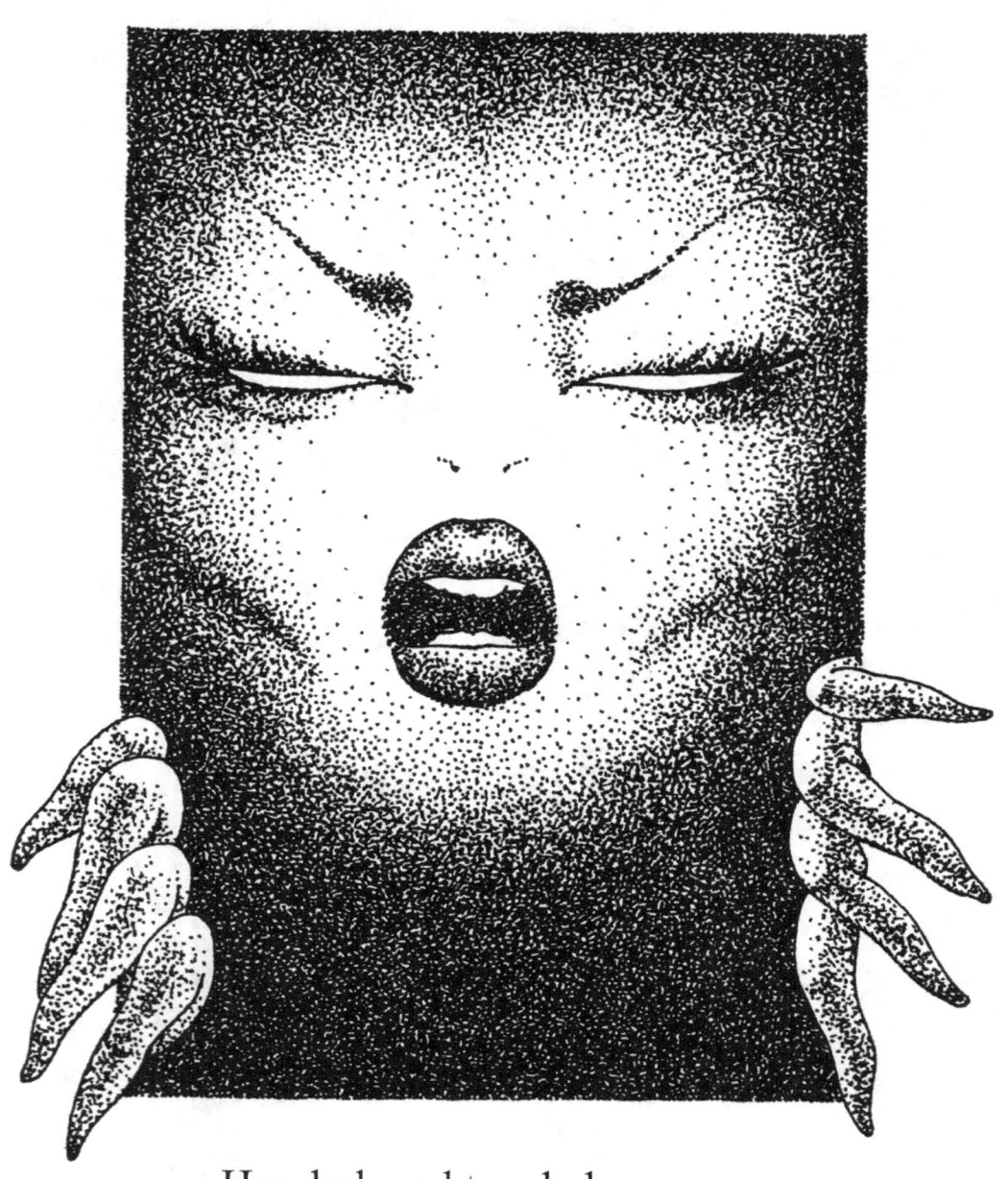

Her dark and tangled memory
Is still tapping at the one small window
In my heart,
Like a clock ticking.

END

www.ingramcontent.com/pod-product-compliance
Lightning Source LLC
Chambersburg PA
CBHW081504170526
45166CB00008B/2554